V&R

KLAUS BEYER

The Aramaic Language

Its Distribution and Subdivisions

Translated from the German
by John F. Healey

VANDENHOECK & RUPRECHT
IN GÖTTINGEN

This volume, which appears in the year of the 600th anniversary of the foundation of Heidelberg University, contains a translation of an updated version of the first chapter, "Die Verbreitung und Gliederung des Aramäischen", of Klaus Beyer's book, *Die aramäischen Texte vom Toten Meer samt den Inschriften aus Palästina, dem Testament Levis aus der Kairoer Genisa, der Fastenrolle und den alten talmudischen Zitaten: Aramaistische Einleitung, Text, Übersetzung, Deutung, Grammatik, Wörterbuch, Deutsch-aramäische Wortliste, Register,* Göttingen: Vandenhoeck & Ruprecht, 1984, pp. 23–76. In the complete German work (abbreviated: *ATTM*) it forms with the second chapter, "Die Entwicklung des Aramäischen" ("The Development of Aramaic": a diachronic account of Aramaic phonology, pp. 77–153), a general introduction from the point of view of Aramaic studies. A preliminary *Ergänzungsheft* to all sections of the German book will appear in 1989. The stimulus for this English edition and the translation were provided by Dr John F. Healey, Lecturer in Semitic Philology in the School of Oriental Studies, University of Durham, England, though the author himself accepts responsibility for the final text.

CIP-Kurztitelaufnahme der Deutschen Bibliothek

Beyer, Klaus:
The Aramaic Language : its distribution and subdivisions /
Klaus Beyer. Transl. from the German by John F. Healey. –
Göttingen : Vandenhoeck und Ruprecht, 1986.

ISBN 3-525-53573-2

Gesetzt aus Times auf Digiset 200 T2
Gesamtherstellung: Hubert & Co., Göttingen.

Contents

Signs and Abbreviations

↗ refers to pages of this English edition, → to pages of the German original (↗ 4). ə stands for a neutral short vowel. ẹ ọ are closed, ę ǫ open vowels (cf. *day-bed*: *dẹ̄-będ*; *mǫttọ̄*). ¯ indicates a long vowel.

AION *Annali dell'Istituto Orientale Universitario di Napoli*
BASOR *Bulletin of the American Schools of Oriental Research* (ASOR)
BiOr *Bibliotheca Orientalis*
BLA BLH H. Bauer und P. Leander, grammars (↗ 8)
BSOAS *Bulletin of the School of Oriental and African Studies*
Bulletin Bulletin d'épigraphie sémitique (↗ 8)
CIS *Corpus Inscriptionum Semiticarum*, vol. 2, Paris 1889 ff. (no.)
Dalman G. Dalman, grammar (↗ 8)
DISO *Dictionnaire des inscriptions sémitiques de l'ouest* (↗ 8)
DJD *Discoveries in the Judaean Desert*, Oxford 1955 ff. (vol. + p.)
ESE M. Lidzbarski, *Ephemeris für semitische Epigraphik*, Giessen 1900–15
J. A. Fitzmyer and D. J. Harrington, *A Manual of Palestinian Aramaic Texts*, Rome 1978
J. B. Frey, *Corpus Inscriptionum Iudaicarum*, 2 vols., Rome 1975, 1952 (no.)
HUCA *Hebrew Union College Annual*
IEJ *Israel Exploration Journal*
IOS *Israel Oriental Studies*
JAOS *Journal of the American Oriental Society*
JEOL *Jaarbericht Ex Oriente Lux*
JJS *Journal of Jewish Studies*
JNES *Journal of Near Eastern Studies*
JSJ *Journal for the Study of Judaism*
JSS *Journal of Semitic Studies*
KAI H. Donner and W. Röllig, *Kanaanäische und aramäische Inschriften*, 3rd ed., Wiesbaden 1971–76, + W. E. Aufrecht, *A Synoptic Concordance of Aramaic Inscriptions* (KAI 201 ff.), Missoula 1975
LXX Septuagint (Greek Old Testament)
NESE R. Degen, in: *Neue Ephemeris für semitische Epigraphik*, Wiesbaden 1972 ff.
RA *Revue d'Assyriologie*
RB *Revue Biblique*
REJ *Revue des Études Juives*
RES *Répertoire d'épigraphie sémitique*, Paris 1900 ff. (no.)
E. Schürer, *Geschichte des jüdischen Volkes im Zeitalter Jesu Christi*, 3 vols., 4th ed., Leipzig 1901–09 / revised and ed. by G. Vermes, F. Millar and M. Black, *The History of the Jewish People in the Age of Jesus Christ*, Edinburgh 1973–1985
H. L. Strack – G. Stemberger, *Einleitung in Talmud und Midrasch*, Munich 1982
TSSI J. C. L. Gibson, *Textbook of Syrian Semitic Inscriptions*, vol. 2: Aramaic Inscriptions, Oxford 1975 (no.)
ZAW *Zeitschrift für die alttestamentliche Wissenschaft*
ZDMG *Zeitschrift der Deutschen Morgenländischen Gesellschaft*

The Most Important Literature

Research on Aramaic to Date

F. Rosenthal, *Die aramaistische Forschung seit Th. Nöldekes Veröffentlichungen*, Leiden 1939, reprint 1964 (5 tables of script and a map).
E. Y. Kutscher, "Aramaic", in: *Current Trends in Linguistics*, ed. T. A. Sebeok, vol. 6, The Hague 1970, 347–412 (continues Rosenthal; 10th–3rd cent. B.C.).
H. J. W. Drijvers, "Syriac and Aramaic", in: *A Basic Bibliography for the Study of the Semitic Languages*, ed. J. H. Hospers, vol. 1, Leiden 1973, 283–335.
J. Teixidor, "Bulletin d'épigraphie sémitique", in: *Syria* from 44 (1967) (texts on hard material; referred to according to "Bulletin" no.).
Tübinger Atlas des Vorderen Orients A VIII–X. B IV–X, Wiesbaden 1977 ff.
Notices of journals and books in *JSJ*, *Orientalia* and *ZAW*.
On the development and dating of the Aramaic script ↗ 9 n. 4.

Grammars Spanning Several Dialects

C. Brockelmann, *Grundriß der vergleichenden Grammatik der semitischen Sprachen*, 2 vols., Berlin 1908, 1913, reprint 1961 ("*GVG*").
S. Moscati (ed.), *An Introduction to the Comparative Grammar of the Semitic Languages*. Phonology and Morphology, Wiesbaden 1964, reprint 1980.
H. Bauer and P. Leander, *Historische Grammatik der hebräischen Sprache des Alten Testaments*, Halle 1922, reprint 1962 ("*BLH*" with page reference).
–, *Grammatik des Biblisch-Aramäischen*, Halle 1927, reprint 1962 ("*BLA*").
E. Brønno, *Studien über hebräische Morphologie und Vokalismus auf Grundlage der Mercatischen Fragmente der zweiten Kolumne der Hexapla des Origenes*, Leipzig 1943, reprint 1966, with G. Janssens, *Studies in Hebrew Historical Linguistics Based on Origen's Secunda*, Louvain 1982.
G. Dalman, *Grammatik des jüdisch-palästinischen Aramäisch*, Leipzig 1905, reprints 1960, 1981.
K. Beyer, *Semitische Syntax im Neuen Testament I*, 2nd ed., Göttingen 1968.

Dictionaries Spanning Several Dialects

C. F. Jean – J. Hoftijzer, *Dictionnaire des inscriptions sémitiques de l'ouest*, Leiden 1965 (10th cent. B.C. to 3rd cent. A.D.; excluding names; "*DISO*").
J. Levy, *Neuhebräisches und chaldäisches Wörterbuch über die Talmudim und Midraschim*, 4 vols., Leipzig 1876–1889, reprint 1963.
–, *Chaldäisches Wörterbuch über die Targumim und einen großen Theil des rabbinischen Schriftthums*, 2 vols., Leipzig 1867–1868, reprint 1959.
G. Dalman, *Aramäisch-Neuhebräisches Handwörterbuch zu Targum, Talmud und Midrasch*, 2nd ed., Frankfurt 1922, reprints 1938, 1967.
W. v. Soden, *Akkadisches Handwörterbuch*, Wiesbaden 1965–1981.
S. Fraenkel, *Die aramäischen Fremdwörter im Arabischen*, Leiden 1886, reprint 1962.
S. A. Kaufman, *The Akkadian Influences on Aramaic*, Chicago 1974.
W. Hinz, *Altiranisches Sprachgut der Nebenüberlieferungen*, Wiesbaden 1975.
For onomastica → 445 n. 1.

For a considerable time after the other Semites[1,2] had expanded, the Aramaeans still remained a small group isolated in a remote region north or south of where they later settled. Only from the 12th cent. B.C. on, after they had greatly increased in number because of favourable circumstances, did they migrate on a large scale into Syria, Mesopotamia and Babylonia.[3] From the 11th cent. B.C. they formed states (especially Sam'al, Arpad, Hamath and Damascus in western Syria and Gozan in north-eastern Syria), taking over from the Phoenicians the alphabetic script (↗ 56), improving it with the use of vowel-letters (↗ 59, → 409) and handing it on about 1000 B.C. to the Israelites, from whom the Moabites, Edomites and Philistines adopted it, and to the Ammonites and Gileadites.[4] From the 8th cent.

---

[1] The eight Semitic language groups are best reduced to four branches: I North Semitic (1. the Syrian/Euphrates dialects [Kiš, Mari, Ebla (2500 B.C.!); parts of Ugaritic (the *š*-causative) and of Ya'udic (↗ 12 n.)]), II East Semitic (2. Babylonian-Assyrian), III West Semitic (3. Canaanite, 4. Aramaic), IV South Semitic (5. Arabic, 6. Ancient North Arabic, 7. South Arabian, 8. Ethiopic). Hamitic (Egyptian + Coptic; Berber, Cushitic and Chadic) is connected originally with Semitic. In the wider context both are related to Indo-Europaean, since these three are the only inflected, i.e. root-modifying, language families in the world. Personal names are generally ancient.

[2] Canaanite is divided into North Canaanite (parts of Ugaritic, the language of the names at Ugarit), East Canaanite (Amorite), West Canaanite (Proto-Byblian, the western area Amarna glosses, Phoenician-Punic [+ the Gezer Calendar]) and South Canaanite (Proto-Sinaitic, Taanach + southern area Amarna glosses, North Hebrew, Ammonite, Moabite, South Hebrew [↗ 34 n.44], Gileadite, Edomite). The languages of the peoples who settled in historical times (Amorites, Israelites, Ammonites, Moabites, Gileadites, Edomites) are more conservative. Canaanite is in the historical period a looser unit than Aramaic, because the Canaanites began to spread out over the arable areas much earlier. See my *Althebräische Grammatik,* Göttingen 1969 (out of print), with the corrections and improvements included in what follows here and → 77–153; W. R. Garr, *Dialect Geography of Syria-Palestine. 1000–586 B.C.,* Philadelphia 1985 (the distribution of 100 linguistic features).

[3] The Aramaeans are first mentioned clearly in Assyrian sources (Tiglath-Pileser I) in 1112 B.C. As a personal name and place-name, however, *'Aram* appears as early as the third millennium B.C. Both the etymology of this name and when and why the Aramaeans began to call themselves by this title remains unknown.

[4] On the development and dating of the Aramaic script see L. G. Herr, *The Scripts of Ancient Northwest Semitic Seals,* Missoula 1978; S. A. Birnbaum, *The Hebrew Scripts,* 2

B.C. on, Aramaic, thanks to its simplicity and flexibility, increasingly superseded Akkadian and Canaanite – a development which was further accelerated by Assyrian and Neo-Babylonian imperial policy and the use of transportation as part of that policy in the 9th–6th cent. B.C. In the time of Jesus Aramaic was spoken throughout the Semitic area apart from where Punic (until the 5th cent. A.D.) and Arabic were used. In the 7th–10th cent. A.D. Aramaic was extensively replaced by Arabic in conjunction with the spread of Islam. It still survives today, however, in a few places.

The history of Aramaic is best divided into three main sections: Old Aramaic, Middle Aramaic and the Modern Aramaic of the present day. The term Middle Aramaic refers to the form of Aramaic which appears in pointed texts. It is essentially reached in the 3rd cent. A.D. with the loss of short unstressed vowels in open syllables (→ 128–136) and continues until the triumph of Arabic.

Old Aramaic

Old Aramaic is the term used to cover Ancient Aramaic, Imperial Aramaic, Old Eastern Aramaic and Old Western Aramaic. All pre-Imperial Aramaic texts are Ancient Aramaic. The boundary between Ancient and Imperial Aramaic is thus provided, the most decisive

---

vols., Leiden 1954, 1971; M. Beit-Arié, *Hebrew Codicology*, Jerusalem 1981; J. Naveh, *The Development of the Aramaic Script*, Jerusalem 1970 (10th–3rd cent. B.C.), + *BASOR* 198 (1970), 32–37 (Mandaic), *IOS* 2 (1972), 293–304 (East Mesopotamian); S. J. Lieberman, "The Aramaic Argillary Script in the Seventh Century", *BASOR* 192 (1968), 25–31; A. C. Klugkist, "The Importance of the Palmyrene Script for our Knowledge of the Development of the Late Aramaic Scripts", in: M. Sokoloff (ed.), *Arameans, Aramaic and the Aramaic Literary Tradition*, Ramat-Gan 1983, 57–74; F. M. Cross, "The Development of the Jewish Scripts", in: *Festschrift W. F. Albright*, London 1961, 133–202, + *DJD* 3 (1962), 217–221 (↗ 20 n. 14); P. T. Daniels, "A Calligraphic Approach to Aramaic Paleography", *JNES* 43 (1984), 55–68. The Old Hebrew/Moabite/Edomite alphabet falls behind the development of the Aramaic alphabet as early as the 9th cent. B.C. and the Ammonite alphabet begins to fall behind in about 750 B.C. The Old Hebrew and Moabite/Edomite alphabets separate from each other about 800 B.C. and Moabite and Edomite about 700 B.C. From the 6th cent. B.C. onwards they were all replaced by the Aramaic alphabet. See most recently L. G. Herr, *BASOR* 238 (1980), 21–34; P. K. McCarter, ibid. 239 (1980), 50. By contrast J. Naveh denies the existence of a special non-Aramaic Ammonite script and so places the evidence about 60 years earlier.

point being around 500 B.C. Lesser breaks around 700 and 200 B.C. separate early and late Ancient Aramaic from each other on the one hand and Achaemenid from post-Achaemenid Imperial Aramaic on the other. Hence both Ancient Aramaic and Imperial Aramaic begin as unified written languages, which dissolve into looser groupings in late Ancient Aramaic and post-Achaemenid Imperial Aramaic. By Old Eastern and Old Western Aramaic are meant the initially unwritten dialects of eastern Syria, Mesopotamia, Babylonia and the eastern Tigris area on the one side and of western Syria and Palestine on the other. These developed into local written languages only after the end of Imperial Aramaic. As the first differences between Eastern and Western Aramaic were already evident in the 9th cent. B.C. (→ 97), the spoken dialects ought to be divided from the beginning, with the boundary running in a north-south direction between Aleppo and the southern Orontes on the one hand and the Euphrates and Palmyra on the other (↗ 40, 55). Because of its great extent, Eastern Aramaic is subdivided into the northern Eastern Aramaic of eastern Syria and Mesopotamia and the southern Eastern Aramaic of Babylonia and the eastern Tigris area.[5] Ancient Aramaic arose on the territory of Western Aramaic and Imperial Aramaic on the territory of southern Eastern Aramaic.

Ancient Aramaic

Ancient Aramaic in written form appeared in the 11th cent. B.C. as the official language of the first Aramaean states. The oldest witnesses to it are inscriptions from northern Syria of the 10th–8th cent. B.C., especially extensive state treaties (Sfire I–III: c.750 B.C.) and royal inscriptions. This early Ancient Aramaic consists of two clearly distinguished and standardized written languages,[6] namely the

---

[5] All the Aramaic dialects with their title beginning with "Old" belong to Old Aramaic. The term "Old" is only used, however, if the dialect in question has a continuation in Middle or even Modern Aramaic, for which "Middle" and "Modern" are then used, as in Old, Middle and Modern Syriac. Further subdivision can be made by the use of "early" and "late". On account of lack of space, only the most recent edition of a particular text is mentioned in the references which follow.

[6] Ancient Aramaic[1]: R. Degen, *Altaramäische Grammatik der Inschriften des 10.–8. Jh. v. Chr.*, Wiesbaden 1969, reprint 1978; *KAI* 201–213, 216–224, 231, 232; *TSSI* 1–12, 15–17; *DISO*: "Aram. Anc.". There are also seals from Byblos (9th cent. B.C.): H. Sey-

original one of western Syria, related orthographically to Phoenician (→ 88 n. 1), which R. Degen described in 1969, and the one further improved in the east, perhaps as early as the 11th cent. B.C. (ס for *ṯ*, corresponding to ז for *ḏ*, and י for *-ḗ*, easing the ambiguity of ש and ה; ו י for medial *ū* and *ī*; etymological writing of assimilated *n* and *l*), which is known only through the inscription from Gozan, but which has influenced the further development of the orthography, though subsequently it did itself disappear. By contrast, the late Ancient Aramaic of the 7th–6th cent. B.C., evidence of which comes from

---

rig, *Syria* 32 (1955), 42 f. (חתם ברק עבד עתרשמן, "Seal of Baraq the servant of ʿAttaršamáyn") and Khorsabad (8th cent. B.C.): J. Naveh (↗ 10 n.) 10 f., ivory from Nimrud (8th cent. B.C.): W. Röllig in: *NESE* 2 (1974), 44–59; Bulletin 1969, 117, an inscription from Meskene (8th cent. B.C.): J. Teixidor, *RA* 77 (1983), 78–80, and above all an inscription of 23 lines of the Aramaean King *Haddyḗṯī* of Gozan on the upper Habur (c. 850 B.C.) with an improved orthography and certain obvious peculiarities (archaic script of the 11th–10th cent. B.C.; 3rd masc. and fem. plur. suffixes ם and ן on singulars; אל instead of על, "over"; נשון, "women"; collective singulars treated as plurals not only after numerals; itp. stem with infixed *t*; jussive with preformative *l-* except after אל, "not!"; qal infinitive already *maqtál*; זי already in use as genitive particle; emphasising *-m*): A. Abou-Assaf, P. Bordreuil and A. R. Millard, *La statue de Tell Fekherye et son inscription bilingue assyro-araméenne*, Paris 1982. In addition the three "Ya'udic" royal inscriptions from Zinjirli in northern Syria (c. 825, 750, 730 B.C.) witness to early Ancient Aramaic: *KAI* 25, 214, 215; *TSSI* –, 13, 14; J. Friedrich, *Phönizisch-punische Grammatik*, Rome 1951, 153–162; P.-E. Dion, *La langue de Ya'udi*, Waterloo/Ontario 1974 and Bulletin 1976, 12; 1979, 11; E. Lipiński, *BiOr* 33 (1976), 232 (מת, "land"); W. R. Garr (↗ 9 n. 2); *DISO*: "Yaod."; ↗ 15; → 80, 89, 97, 104, 148, 414, 416. So-called Ya'udic is, in fact, not an archaic form of Aramaic – in that case "his hands" (gen./acc. dual) would have been ידו **yadáw* (→ 83 n. 2), later ידוה *yadáwhī*, rather than ידיה *yadḗhī/ū* (→ 150 f.) – but a mixture of the local North Semitic dialect (↗ 9 n. 1) of the old-established population (*KAI* 24: 10) of "Ya'udi"/Śam'āl (about 180 km north of Ugarit) and Phoenician and the Aramaic of the immigrants. Un-Aramaic are: the (complete?) change of *aw* > *ọ̄* (משב, "throne"!) and *ay* > *ẹ̄* (?; from the consonantal point of view on the other hand Ya'udic is Aramaic – cf. ק *ğ*); the absence of the article and the emphatic state (certainly North Semitic influence); the masc. plur. nominative ending *-ū* (dual *-ẹ̄*, since *-ā* = feminine ending), in genitive/accusative *-ī* (dual *-ẹ̄*) without distinction of absolute and construct state (certainly North Semitic); the afformative of the imperfect of 2nd and 3rd masc. plur. *-ū*, fem. plur. *-nā* (or *-n*? → 147); אנכ(י), "I"; בית absolute, "house"; קיר, "city"; מקם, "place"; אם, "if"; הן, "behold"; גם, "also"; אמן, "truly"; as also the lack of marking of stressed final long vowels: זן *dẹnā́*, ז *dī*, קן *qanā́*. Yet Aramaic clearly predominates. Since an archaic form of Phoenician (*KAI* 24; c. 825 B.C.) as well as Ancient Aramaic (*KAI* 216–221; *TSSI* 15–17; c. 730 B.C.) were available in Ya'udi as written languages and Ya'udic is not a mixture of these two, it seems to have been actually spoken during the transition to Aramaic or at least to have been used as a sacred language.

all over the Near East, broke up gradually into local written languages. The orthography of the Hermopolis Papyri from Egypt (just before 500 B.C.) is thus quite irregular.[7] Aramaic had already in the

---

[7] Ancient Aramaic[2]:

3 short inscriptions from Deir ʿAlla (c. 700 B.C.): J. Hoftijzer and G. van der Kooij, *Aramaic Texts from Deir ʿAlla,* Leiden 1976, 267, cf. J. A. Hackett, *The Balaam Text from Deir ʿAllā,* Chico 1984, (the Balaam text is a hieratic mixture of archaic South Canaanite and spoken Aramaic, cf. Ya'udic and Neo-Hebrew).

2 bronze dishes from Luristan (c. 700, 600 B.C.): Bulletin 1967, 72 (= *TSSI* 12), 73.

2 tomb inscriptions from Nerab in northern Syria (c. 700 B.C.): *KAI* 225, 226; *TSSI* 18, 19; cf. W. R. Garr (↗ 9 n. 2) 42 (תנצר/י paʿʿel); S. Parpola, *Orientalia* 54 (1985).

Debt-note from Nineveh (the oldest dated Aramaic text: 674 B.C.): *CIS* 39; L. Delaporte (↗ below) no. 23.

The Aššur letter (from Babylonia to Aššur; c. 650 B.C.): *KAI* 233; *TSSI* 20.

7 debt-notes from Aššur (no. 4: 659 B.C.; the rest: second half of the 7th cent. B.C.): M. Lidzbarski, *Altaramäische Urkunden aus Assur,* Leipzig 1921, 15–20, + H. Freydank, *Altorientalische Forschungen* 2 (1975), 133–135; E. Lipiński, *Studies in Aramaic Inscriptions and Onomastics* I, Leuven 1975, 83–113; F. M. Fales, *Aramaic Epigraphs on Clay Tablets from the Neo-Assyrian Period,* Rome 1986.

Mutual agreement of unknown origin (635 B.C.): P. Bordreuil, *Semitica* 23 (1973), 95–102; Bulletin 1979, 160; F. M. Fales, op. cit.

5 debt-notes from Tell Halaf or the surrounding country (second half of the 7th cent. B.C.): *NESE* 1, 49–57: E. Lipiński, op. cit., 114–142; F. M. Fales, op. cit.

24 debt-notes from the Gozan-Ḫarran area (7th cent. B.C.): E. Lipiński, in: *Biblical Archaeology Today. Proceedings of the International Congress on Biblical Archaeology Jerusalem April 1984,* Jerusalem 1985, 340–348 (preliminary report).

4 ostraca from Philistia (7th cent. B.C.): J. Naveh, *IEJ* 35 (1985), 19 f.

Ostracon from Egypt (7th cent. B.C.): Aimé-Giron (↗ 16 n.) 2.

2 papyrus fragments from Egypt (7th cent. B.C.): *ESE* 3, 128 f. = *RES* 1791; *NESE* 2, 65–70 with E. Lipiński, *BiOr* 37 (1980), 6 f.

Annotations on Assyrian and Babylonian cuneiform tablets (7th–6th cent. B.C.): L. Delaporte, *Épigraphes araméens,* Paris 1912; F. Vattioni, *Augustinianum* 10 (1970), 493–532; 11 (1971), 187–190; Bulletin 1971, 27; 1973, 141–144; A. R. Millard, *Iraq* 45 (1983), 107 f.; M. Stol, *Zeitschrift für Assyriologie* 73 (1983), 298; F. M. Fales, op. cit.

Inscription against tax evasion from Syria(?) (c. 600 B.C.): E. Lipiński, op. cit. 77–82, with F. M. Fales, *Oriens Antiquus* 16 (1977) 41–68: 65 f.

Letter of the Canaanite king Adon to the Pharaoh (c. 600 B.C.): *KAI* 266; *TSSI* 21; B. Porten, *Biblical Archaeologist* 44 (1981), 36–52; Porten-Yardeni (↗ 16 n.) no. 1.

Loan (571/570 B.C.): *KAI* 227; *TSSI* 22.

Lease from Egypt (515 B.C.): A. Dupont-Sommer, *Mémoires présentés ... à l'Académie des Inscriptions et Belles-Lettres* XIV 2 (1944), 61–106; J. J. Koopmans, *Aramäische Chrestomathie,* Leiden 1962, No. 19; cf. P. Grelot, *Documents araméens d'Égypte,* Paris 1972, 71–75.

3 deeds from Elephantine (end of the 6th cent. B.C.): Cowley (↗ 15 n. 10) 49 + *NESE* 3, 15–28 + B. Porten, *BASOR* 258 (1985), 48–51; Cowley 52; *NESE* 2, 74–78.

8th cent. B.C. become the *lingua franca* of the Near East: between 735 and 732 B.C. a Phoenician from Tyre writes a non-extant Aramaic letter to the Assyrian king Tiglath-Pileser III (H. W. F. Saggs, *Iraq* 17 [1955], 130, 3–7), in 701 B.C. the ambassadors of the Assyrian king Sennacherib and the Judaean king Hezekiah negotiate in Aramaic before the walls of Jerusalem so that the people of Jerusalem do not understand (2 Kings 18:26) and c. 600 B.C. a Canaanite king, Adon, writes an Aramaic letter to the Egyptian Pharaoh.[8] Aramaic was influenced at first principally by Akkadian, then from the 5th cent. B.C. by Persian and from the 3rd cent. B.C. onwards by Greek,[9] as well as by Hebrew, especially in Palestine.

Imperial Aramaic

About 500 B.C. Darius I (522–486 B.C.) made the Aramaic used by the Achaemenid imperial administration (there being no question of any other Aramaic) into the official language of the western half of the Persian Empire. This co-called Imperial Aramaic (the oldest dated example, Cowley 1 from Egypt, belonging to 495 B.C.) is based on an otherwise unknown written form of Ancient Aramaic from

---

Tomb inscription from Egypt (end of the 6th cent. B.C.): Aimé-Giron (↗ 16 n.) 110 bis; A. Dupont-Sommer, *Syria* 33 (1956), 79–87; cf. P. Grelot, op. cit., 335 f.

Hermopolis Papyri (8 private letters of Aramaean soldiers of Syro-Mesopotamian origin from Egypt; shortly before 500 B.C.): *TSSI* 27; Porten-Yardeni (↗ 16 n.).

Numerous names and measures on seals, weights, vessels, etc.

S. Segert, *Altaramäische Grammatik* (10th–2nd cent. B.C.), Leipzig 1975, reprint 1983, with R. Degen, *Göttingische Gelehrte Anzeigen* 231 (1979), 8–51; *DISO*: "Aram. Emp."; W. Kornfeld, *Onomastica Aramaica aus Ägypten*, Vienna 1978.

[8] In the 14th cent. B.C. the Canaanite princes of the city-states in Palestine wrote the so-called Amarna letters (↗ 9 n. 2) to the Pharaoh in Akkadian (the *lingua franca* of the Near East in the 2nd millennium B.C.; ↗ 9 n. 1). Ugarit also (destroyed in c. 1200 B.C.) conducted its external correspondence in Akkadian, while c. 2500 B.C. at Ebla Sumerian was used for this purpose, since Sumerian was the *lingua franca* in the 3rd millennium B.C.

[9] → 99, 103; Kaufman (↗ 8); Hinz (↗ 8); S. Krauss, *Griechische und lateinische Lehnwörter im Talmud, Midrasch und Targum*, 2 vols., Berlin 1898, 1899, reprint 1964, with D. Sperber, *Bar Ilan Annual* (English section) 14/15 (1977), 9–60; 16/17 (1979), 9–30; D. Sperber, *A Dictionary of Greek and Latin Legal Terms in Rabbinic Literature*, Ramat-Gan 1984; cf. also A. Schlatter, *Verkanntes Griechisch*, Gütersloh 1900; S. Lieberman, *Greek in Jewish Palestine*, New York 1965; J. N. Sevenster, *Do You Know Greek? How much Greek could the first Jewish Christians have known?* Leiden 1968.

Babylonia, with the following features: *n* was not assimilated (→ 91); "daughter" is *bàrat*; the infinitive of the derived stems is formed without *ma-* (→ 150); the afʿel of יטב, "be well", is formed with *aw* in the manner of Eastern Aramaic; the 3rd fem. plur. of the personal pronoun, suffix and verb (in line with the demonstrative pronoun) is replaced by the masc.; the imperfect with suffixes is replaced by the energic II or I with suffixes; the 3rd plur. object suffixes are replaced by the personal pronouns; שנת (without ב), "in the year"; as an alternative to the perfect to enliven the narrative without changing the meaning the ("long") imperfect was used (as early as the 8th cent. B.C.: *KAI* 202A:11,15; 215:4f.); the participle served for historic present; word-order was free and the construct state could be avoided through use of the relative pronoun *dī* (also with anticipatory suffix). An origin in a spoken dialect of Eastern Aramaic is out of the question, since these dialects already had later, specific traits of Eastern Aramaic. Also in orthography Imperial Aramaic has a liking for historical forms (→ 98, 143, 148, 150, 415). Alphabet, orthography, morphology, pronunciation, vocabulary, syntax (including the Persian object-infinitive word-order) and style are highly standardized. Only the formularies of the private documents and the Proverbs of Ahiqar have preserved an older tradition of sentence structure and style. Imperial Aramaic immediately replaced Ancient Aramaic as a written language and, with slight modifications, it remained the official, commercial and literary language of the Near East until gradually, beginning with the fall of the Persian Empire (331 B.C.) and ending in the 4th cent. A.D., it was replaced by Greek, Persian, the eastern and western dialects of Aramaic and Arabic, though not without leaving its traces in the written form of most of these.

In its original Achaemenid form, Imperial Aramaic is found in texts of the 5th–3rd cent. B.C.[10] These come mostly from Egypt and

---

[10] Imperial Aramaic[1] (Unless otherwise noted, the texts were written in Egypt in the 5th cent. B.C.):

A.E.Cowley, Aramaic Papyri of the Fifth Century B.C., Oxford 1923, reprint 1967: from Elephantine, 78 private contracts, letters and lists; the Wisdom of Ahiqar (new edition of Ahiqar 79–223: J.M.Lindenberger, *The Aramaic Proverbs of Ahiqar*, Baltimore 1983; with northern Old Eastern Aramaic influence: ↗ 31); narrative of Bar Puneš (71); Bisitun inscription (new edition by J.C.Greenfield and B.Porten in *Corpus Inscriptionum Iranicarum* I 5, 1982); end of the tomb inscription of Naqš-i Rustam (N. Sims-Williams, *BSOAS* 44 [1981], 1–7: Bisitun 52–56 = *CII* 66–70); from Edfu, Saqqara etc. (81–85; mostly 3rd cent. B.C.).

N. Aimé-Giron, *Textes araméens d'Égypte,* Cairo 1931 (Nos. 1–112; on 5–24 cf. R. A. Bowman, *American Journal of Semitic Languages and Literatures* 58 [1941], 302–313) + *Bulletin de l'Institut Français d'archéologie orientale* 38 (1939), 1–63 (nos. 113–121) + *Annales du Service des antiquités de l'Égypte* 39 (1939), 339–363 (Nos. 122–124); 40 (1941), 433–460 (Nos. 125 ff.): inscriptions, a journal of 472/471 B.C., lists, letters, etc. mostly badly damaged (5th–3rd cent. B.C.).

E. G. Kraeling, *The Brooklyn Museum Aramaic Papyri,* New Haven 1953: from Elephantine, 14 private contracts, 1 letter and 2 unclear texts.

G. R. Driver, *Aramaic Documents of the Fifth Century B.C.,* Oxford 1954, reprint 1968; Abridged and Revised Edition, 1957, reprint 1965, + J. D. Whitehead, *JNES* 37 (1978), 119–140: some 20 letters from Susa or Babylon (c. 410 B.C.) on leather and with Demotic annotations of the Persian satrap in Egypt, Aršama (+ Cowley 26), and senior Persian officials.

3 letters from the museum of Padua: *TSSI* 28; J. A. Fitzmyer, *A Wandering Aramean,* Missoula 1979, 219–230.

Elephantine papyrus from the Egyptian Museum in Berlin (c. 370 B.C.): J. Naveh and S. Shaked, *JAOS* 91 (1971), 379–382, = *NESE* 1, 9–22; Z. Shunnar, in: F. Altheim and R. Stiehl, *Christentum am Roten Meer* II, Berlin 1973, 277–289, 379–395; D. Golomb, *BASOR* 217 (1975), 49–53.

Further Elephantine papyri: Cowley 80 + *RES* 248 + 1798; *NESE* 2, 71–74; 3, 28–31; *Semitica* 27 (1977), 103 f.

4 fragmentary letters from Saqqara: *RES* 1808–1810 = B. Porten, *Semitica* 33 (1983), 89–100; *RES* 1789; *RES* 1790 (all 5th cent. B.C.); RES 1807 (3rd cent. B.C.).

J. B. Segal, *Aramaic Texts from North Saqqara,* London 1983 (pagan).

Letter from el-Hibeh (c. 350 B.C.): E. Bresciani, *Aegyptus* 39 (1959), 3–8; J. T. Milik, ibid. 40 (1960), 79–81; J. Hoftijzer, *Vetus Testamentum* 12 (1962), 341 f.

B. Porten and A. Yardeni, *Textbook of Aramaic Documents from Ancient Egypt. Newly Copied, Edited and Translated into Hebrew and English,* vol. 1: *Letters* (mostly from Cowley and Driver), with an *Appendix: Aramaic Letters from the Bible,* Jerusalem 1986.

List (first half of 3rd cent. B.C.): E. Bresciani, *Atti dell'Accademia Nazionale dei Lincei* 17 (1962), 258–264; J. Naveh, *AION* 16 (1966), 35 f.

40 deeds of sale, written in Samaria and badly damaged, from a cave north of Jericho (375–335 B.C.): F. M. Cross, *Eretz Israel* 18 (1985), 7*–17* (pap. 1); id., in: P. W. Lapp and N. L. Lapp (eds.), *Discoveries in the Wadi ed-Daliyeh,* Cambridge/Mass. 1974, 17–29 (preliminary report on the rest).

4 silver vessels (c. 400 B.C.): *TSSI* 25; Bulletin 1972, 145; cf. E. A. Knauf, *Ismael,* Wiesbaden 1985, 104 f.

17 badly damaged tomb inscriptions from Sheikh-Fadl (c. 460 B.C.): N. Giron, *Ancient Egypt* 1923, 38–43 = J. J. Koopmans, *Aramäische Chrestomathie,* Leiden 1962, no. 15.

10 stone inscriptions from Egypt: *CIS* 122 = *KAI* 267 = *TSSI* 23; *CIS* 123 = *KAI* 268; *CIS* 141 = *KAI* 269 = *TSSI* 24; *CIS* 142 = *KAI* 272; *CIS* 143; Aimé-Giron 114; *ESE* 2, 221–223 = *RES* 438 + 1806; *RES* 1788, 1818, 1819.

15 inscriptions from Abydos (5th–3rd cent. B.C.): *ESE* 3, 93–116 + W. Kornfeld, *Anzeiger der Österr. Akademie der Wissenschaften* 115 (1978), 193–204.

10 inscriptions from Wadi es-Saba Rigaleh in Egypt: *CIS* 135, 136; *RES* 960–962, 1787; also from Akhmim: RES 1817 (all 5th–4th cent. B.C.).

9 Jewish tomb inscriptions from Edfu (4th cent. B.C.): *NESE* 3, 59–66; Bulletin 1976, 164f.

3 Jewish tomb inscriptions from the necropolis of Alexandria (c. 300 B.C.); Frey 1424–1426.

Name list from Egypt (3rd cent. B.C.): *ESE* 2, 243–248 = *RES* 1794.

11 stone inscriptions from Asia Minor, the first six from Cilicia (5th–4th cent. B.C.; *RES* 954: 3rd cent. B.C.): *KAI* 258 = *TSSI* 33 = Bulletin 1979, 161; *KAI* 259 = *TSSI* 34; *KAI* 261 = *TSSI* 35; *KAI* 278 = *TSSI* 36; A. Dupont-Sommer, *Jahrbuch für kleinasiatische Forschung* 1 (1950/51), 45–47, 108; *KAI* 260 (+ Lydian); *CIS* 109 = *KAI* 262 (+ Greek); *TSSI* 37; Bulletin 1979, 162 + *Semitica* 29 (1979), 101–103 (+ Greek and Lycian); *ESE* 3, 65f. = *RES* 954 = Bulletin 1976, 168 (+ Greek); cf. E. Lipiński, *Studies in Aramaic Inscriptions and Onomastics* I, Leuven 1975, 146–208.

Weight from Asia Minor: *CIS* 108 = *KAI* 263; H. Chantraine, *ZDMG* 125 (1975), 265f.: 31.808 kg.

Coins from Cilicia (4th cent. B.C.): A. Vattioni, *Augustinianum 11* (1971), 70–78.

24 inscriptions from Teima and region in the Arabian desert (c. 400 B.C.): *NESE* 2, 79–98 (1: *CIS* 113; *KAI* 228; *TSSI* 30); A. Livingstone, *Atlal* 7 (1983), 104–111.

Annotations on Babylonian cuneiform tablets (5th–4th cent. B.C.): ↗ 13 n. 7; L. Jacob-Rost and H. Freydank, *Forschungen und Berichte* 14 (1972), 7–35.

Annotations on Elamite cuneiform tablets: R. T. Hallock, *Persepolis Fortification Tablets*, Chicago 1969, 82.

163 almost identical administrative texts from Persepolis (479–435 B.C.): R. A. Bowman, *Aramaic Ritual Texts from Persepolis*, Chicago 1970, + J. Naveh and S. Shaked, *Orientalia* 42 (1973), 445–457; Bulletin 1974, 152.

Hundreds of more or less damaged ostraca, mostly private letters especially from Egypt and Palestine, though also from Babylonia (5th–3rd cent. B.C.): only partly published, cf. J. Naveh (↗ 10 n.) 37–40, 43–45; Bulletin under "Araméen"; ↗ 37; 40 n. 52; → 103 n.

The five inscriptions of the Indian king, Aśoka (reigned 268–233 B.C.), from Afghanistan and Pakistan are clumsy translations of religious edicts: 1. Taxila: *KAI* 273; Bulletin 1973, 170; 2. Pul-i Darunta near Kabul (+ Indic): F. Altheim, *Weltgeschichte Asiens im griechischen Zeitalter* I, Halle 1947, 25–43 = *Festschrift O. Eissfeldt*, Halle 1947, 29–46; W. B. Henning, *BSOAS* 13 (1949/50), 80–88; 3. Kandahar I (+ Greek; intact): *KAI* 279; Bulletin 1969, 118; 4. Kandahar II (+ Indic): Bulletin 1969, 119; 5. Laghman valley: Bulletin 1971, 119; 1979, 162 bis.

Silver tablet (3rd cent. B.C.): Bulletin 1967, 74; 1968, 18; 1973, 159.

Inscription from Kerak in Moab (c. 275 B.C.): J. T. Milik, *Studii Biblici Franciscani Liber Annuus* 9 (1958/59), 331–341; 10 (1959/60), 156.

Inscription from al-Jawf, half way between Cairo and Kuwait (2nd cent. B.C.): C. C. Torrey, *JAOS* 54 (1934), 29–33.

Inscription from Dan near Hermon (+ Greek; c. 200 B.C.): A. Biran, *IEJ* 26 (1976), 204f. (נדר זילס לא[להא ... נדר] [...] "[...] Soilos vowed to the god [in Dan a vow]"; Old East Jordanian?: ↗ 35f.).

Extensive papyrus with cultic texts in Demotic script (4th cent. B.C.: → 101f. 420): S. P. Vleeming and J. W. Wesselius, *BiOr* 39 (1982), 501–509; *JEOL* 28 (1983–84), 110–140; id., *Studies in Papyrus Amherst 63*, vol. 1ff., Amsterdam 1985ff.; C. F. Nims and R. C. Steiner, *JAOS* 103 (1983), 261–274; *JNES* 43 (1984), 89–114 ($\bar{g}$ > $\acute{g}$ in 7th

especially from the Jewish military colony of Elephantine, which existed at least from 530 (see Cowley 30:13; in fact probably from about 580: ↗ 40 n.52) to 399 B.C. (latest known date: Kraeling 13). The script and language of Imperial Aramaic are so unified that the place of origin of a text is only betrayed by the frequency of Persian, Egyptian, Anatolian (i.e. from Asia Minor), Akkadian or Indic loanwords and names or alternatively by mistakes or infelicities of language which show, as in the inscriptions from Asia Minor and northern India, that Aramaic is not the mother-tongue of the writer. Nor did the end of the Persian imperial administration in 331 B.C. alter things immediately. Only about a century later did the script, orthography and language of the individual areas begin to develop more and more differences, under the influence of the spoken dialects. Hence it is advisable to subdivide Imperial Aramaic geographically from the 2nd cent. B.C.[11] Its area of influence had, however, diminished meanwhile, since in the 4th cent. B.C. in Syria/Mesopotamia and in the 3rd cent. B.C. in Egypt and northern Palestine it had been

---

cent. B.C.! → 101); *RB* 92 (1985), 60–81; K.-Th. Zauzich, *Enchoria* 13 (1985), 126–132 (cf. G. Vittmann, *Göttinger Miszellen* 88 [1985], 63–68).

Numerous inscriptions on seals, coins, weights, vessels, mummies, coffins and other objects.

B. Porten, *Archives from Elephantine. The Life of an Ancient Jewish Military Colony*, Berkeley 1968; B. Porten and J.C. Greenfield, *Jews of Elephantine and Arameans of Syene. Fifty Aramaic Texts with Hebrew and English Translations*, Jerusalem 1974 + *JNES* 41 (1982), 123–131; 42 (1983), 279–284; *RB* 90 (1983), 563–575; *Festschrift D.N. Freedman*, Winona Lake 1983, 527–544; *BASOR* 252 (1983), 35–46; 258 (1985), 41–52; R. Yaron, *Introduction to the Law of the Aramaic Papyri*, Oxford 1961, + *RB* 77 (1970), 408–416; Y. Muffs, *Studies in the Aramaic Legal Papyri from Elephantine*, Leiden 1969, reprint 1973; B.A. Levine, "On the Origins of the Aramaic Legal Formulary at Elephantine", in: *Festschrift M. Smith*, Leiden 1975, III 37–54; P. Grelot, *Documents araméens d'Égypte. Introduction, traduction, présentation*, Paris 1972 + RB 82 (1975), 288–292.

P. Leander, *Laut- und Formenlehre des Ägyptisch-Aramäischen*, Göteborg 1928, reprint 1966; S. Segert (↗ 14 n.); *DISO*: "Aram. Emp."; W. Kornfeld, *Onomastica Aramaica aus Ägypten*, Wien 1978, with E. Lipiński, *BiOr* 37 (1980), 5–10; M.H. Silverman, *Religious Values in the Jewish Proper Names at Elephantine*, Neukirchen 1985; E. Y. Kutscher, "Aramaic" (↗ 8) 361–412; → 407–497 "Grammatik".

A few of the texts from Egypt published by J. Leibovitsch, E. Bresciani and J. Teixidor (*TSSI* 29) are modern forgeries: J. Naveh, *JNES* 27 (1968), 317–325; M.H. Silverman, ibid. 28 (1969), 192–196; Bulletin 1975, 139.

[11] This post-Achaemenid Imperial Aramaic is subsumed under the title "Imperial Aramaic²".

superseded by Greek. The retention of Imperial Aramaic in northwest Arabia, Judaea, Palmyra, Babylonia and Parthia serves to underline national independence against the Seleucids and Romans and cultural autonomy against Hellenism. That an older language or linguistic stratum should serve as the written language is a regular feature among the Semites. In Judaea around the time of Christ Middle Hebrew, Neo-Hebrew, Hasmonaean and Old Judaean were all used side by side for the different types of literature.

Biblical Aramaic includes Ezra 4:8–6:18; 7:12–26 (written in the 4th cent. B.C.); Dan 2:4b–7:28 (finished 164 B.C.); Gen 31:47; Jer 10:11. These texts were originally produced in Achaemenid Imperial Aramaic. However, since the Masoretic consonantal text of the Old Testament (Biblia Hebraica) was first definitively established along with the canon in the 1st cent. A.D., later orthographic conventions and grammatical forms (as well as a few Hebraisms) were able to penetrate the text (-*ọ̄*- without ו; אלין, "these"; assimilated *n* without נ; ס for **ś*; *y* > *ʾ*; אנון, אנין, "them"; ד, "which"; reflexive prefix הת; imperfect 3rd fem. plur. ישכנן, להוין; accusative particle ית; מ, "from", even before words not beginning with *n*), while the fragments from Qumran (→ 301; before 68 A.D.) show the usual Hasmonaean orthography of their time. Hence Biblical Aramaic must be dealt with separately.[12]

---

[12] *BLA*; S. Segert (↗ 14 n.); F. Rosenthal, *A Grammar of Biblical Aramaic*, 4th ed., Wiesbaden 1974; L. Díez Merino, *La biblia babilónica*, Madrid 1975 (list of all manuscripts of the Old Testament with Babylonian pointing); S. Morag, "Biblical Aramaic in Geonic Babylonia. The Various Schools", in: *Festschrift H.J. Polotsky*, Jerusalem 1964, 117–131; S. Mandelkern, *Veteris Testamenti Concordantiae Hebraicae atque Chaldaicae*, 2nd ed., Berlin 1925, reprints 1955, 1971, 1312–1348; L. Köhler-W. Baumgartner, *Lexicon in Veteris Testamenti libros*, 2nd ed., Leiden 1958, 1045–1138, 195*–208*; E. Vogt, *Lexicon linguae aramaicae Veteris Testamenti*, Rome 1971; E. Y. Kutscher, "Aramaic" (↗ 8) 375–383, 399–404; K. Koch, *Das Buch Daniel* (Erträge der Forschung), Darmstadt 1980; J. C. H. Lebram, *Das Buch Daniel* (Zürcher Bibelkommentare), Zürich 1984. The Biblical Aramaic vocabulary, including the Qumran readings, is fully covered in the dictionary (→ 500), in which the accompanying transliterations represent the Hasmonaean pronunciation (→ 502). The Palestinian and Babylonian vocalizations (similar respectively to those of the Galilean and Babylonian Targums), finalized in the 10th cent. A.D., are based on Middle Aramaic, but have also preserved older elements (→ 146) and tend to Hebraize (↗ 25). Biblical Aramaic was imitated in the Megillath Antiochus (c. 700 A.D.), ed. M. Z. Kaddari, *Bar Ilan Annual* 1 (Jerusalem 1963), 81–105 (text); 2 (1964), 178–214 (grammar); cf. Dalman 7f.; Schürer I 158f./116; Strack-Stemberger 302f.

Hasmonaean is the written language of Jerusalem and Judaea under the Hasmonaeans (142–37 B.C.). Its emergence is clearly connected with the achievement of independence for Judaea and the beginning of the Hasmonaean era in 142 B.C. (Schürer I 242/190). It ends with the Hasmonaeans in 37 B.C. and in its place Greek[13] comes to the fore as the official language with Old Judaean for private writings (↗ 35), while for theological works only Hebrew remained in use (↗ 34 n.44). Only the formularies of the private documents remain Hasmonaean until 135 A.D. (like the corresponding Babylonian Documentary Aramaic down to the later period). Hasmonaean is attested primarily in the Aramaic theological literature from Qumran (→ 157–303; excluding the Testament of Levi from the Cairo Geniza and the two oldest Enoch manuscripts) and the contemporary inscriptions (→ 328–330). In addition one can mention the private documents from the Judaean desert (→ 304–323; 1st cent. B.C. –135 A.D.) and (with some qualification) the sentences quoted in the Mishna (2nd cent. A.D.) and Tosefta (3rd cent. A.D.) from private documents (→ 324–327). Finally Hasmonaean is attested in the older layer of Babylonian and Galilean Targumic and Babylonian Documentary Aramaic (↗ 24 n.19). The Jewish "square" script was used in its two forms as book-hand (mostly in literary texts) and cursive official script (mostly in inscriptions and archival documents).[14] Hasmonaean is quite distinct from Achaemenid Imperial Aramaic: even unaccented final *-ā* (→ 123) and medial *ọ* (→ 414) are often represented in writing. At the end of a word an unpronounced א is sometimes added to the vowel-letters ה ו י (→ 411). ז for **ḏ* is only found in the pronouns in early texts (→ 415, 425); ס already appears for **ś́* repeatedly in Targum Job (written c. 50 A.D.). Assimilated **n* is

[13] From 37 B.C. to 66 A.D. (Herod and successors) there is only Greek coinage (→ 329); ↗ 14 n.9; 40. On the other hand, of the persons named on Jerusalem ossuaries (→ 339), only about a sixth had no Semitic names.

[14] The oldest stages of the square script are: pre-Hasmonaean 250–142 B.C.; Hasmonaean 142–37 B.C.; Herodian 37 B.C.–70 A.D.; post-Herodian 70–135 A.D. The usual book-hand in the literary texts is very regular and easily legible (block capitals). By contrast the administrative script is more or less cursive; its distinctive marks are: א with special final form, מ ם ס mostly alike, frequent ligatures (i.e. joins between two letters, at least one being shortened); at the same time the letters and ligatures even within the same piece of text can have quite distinct forms, while on the other hand distinct letters end up looking alike (so that a vertical stroke could indicate ר י ז ו ד). Book-hand and cursive can also be mixed together.

increasingly not written (→ 91). In Judaean, the colloquial language of Jerusalem and Judaea (↗ 38), originate the development of *y* > ʾ between a long and a long or short vowel (→ 418), the frequent reduction *ā* > *ọ̄* (→ 137), the 3rd plur. fem. of personal pronoun, suffix and verb (↗ 15), דן *dẹn*, "this", ד *da*, "which, that", the accusative particle ית and the diminishing use of the historic present and free word-order (↗ 15). Also people would not have been able to differentiate strictly the Hasmonaean consonants without the support of the Judaean colloquial. Old Judaean, which ousted Hasmonaean as the Aramaic written language in 37 B.C. except in private documents, is clearly distinguished, like Jewish Old Palestinian (↗ 36) generally, from Imperial Aramaic: the ending of the emphatic state *-ā́* is written with ה and **ś* with ס; assimilated **n* is not written, nor sometimes medial *ẹ̄* and *ọ̄*; the 3rd person imperfect of הוי, "to be", is again formed with *y-* (→ 98 n.1) and the central part of a letter is introduced by (י)ד, "(Communication) that", instead of כען, כע(נ)ת, "now". Naturally these different written forms of Aramaic influenced each other (having also the "square" script in common), at first only a little, but in the Hasmonaean private documents from the Second Jewish Revolt (132–135 A.D.) the Old Judaean influence is already quite strong; the South-east Judaean plur. suffix for "his" ה *-ọ̄́h* also appears (→ 117). Pure Hasmonaean is thus provided only by the texts which were written down between 142 and 37 B.C. (→ 156).

Babylonian Targumic is found in the consonantal text of the Babylonian Targum to Gen-Deut (Onqelos) and to Josh-Mal (Jonathan) which is already attested for Nehardea (northern Babylonia) before 259 A.D., was finally established in the 5th cent. A.D. and later had definitive pointing and Masora added to it.[15] Like Galilean

---

[15] Most recent edition of the Babylonian Targum: A. Sperber, *The Bible in Aramaic*, 3 vols., Leiden 1959–1962 (unsatisfactory on account of lack of reference to the most important manuscripts and many mistakes: A. Díez Macho, in: *Festschrift P. Kahle*, Berlin 1968, 62–78, and *JSJ* 6 (1975), 217–236); M. Aberbach and B. Grossfeld, *Targum Onkelos to Genesis. A Critical Analysis together with an English Translation*, New York 1982; I. Drazin, *Targum Onkelos to Deuteronomy. An English Translation of the Text with Analysis and Commentary*, New York 1982; E. Levine, *The Aramaic Version of Jonah*, Jerusalem 1975 (text, translation, commentary). Genuine Babylonian Targum fragments: L. Díez Merino, *La biblia babilónica. Deuteronomium*, Barcelona 1975; J. R. Florit, *La biblia babilónica. Profetas Posteriores*, Barcelona 1977, + *Anuario de Filologia* 4 (1978), 283–303; 6 (1980), 291–322; *Estudios bíblicos* 40 (1982), 127–158 (to be continued); a magic bowl (↗ 33 n.40); the rhyming poems on Ex 15 and 20 ed. P. Kahle,

Targumic, it is a mixture of Hasmonaean (most significantly, the ending of the emphatic masc. plur. is *-ayyắ* and the only form used for the 3rd person imperfect preformative is *y-*), in which the original Targum was composed, and Jewish Old Babylonian (↗ 33). (Like the Masoretic consonantal text of the Old Testament [established in the 1st cent. A. D.], the Mishna [finalised about 200 A. D.] and the formularies of the private documents [↗ 25], the Hasmonaean Targum had reached Babylonia from Palestine in the 2nd–3rd cent. A. D. [→ 143].) Hence certain Hasmonaean orthographic conventions, sounds, forms and words were systematically replaced with the Jewish Old Babylonian equivalents: י for *ẹ*; ס for **ś*; medial **áy* > *á*; some pronouns; plural for dual; imperfect for jussive; *lā* for *ʾal*, "not!"; 3rd person imperfect of הוי, "to be", with *yẹ-* for *lẹ-*; infinitive qal of I*y* verbs with *mẹ̄-* for *mọ̄-*; passive participle of the pa"el *maqọttál*; בת for ברת, "daughter", in construct; אדן, "ear", and טפר, "claw", following *qutl* instead of *qitl*; *ḥangín*, "festivals", and *gaḏpắ*, *ganpắ*, "wing" (→ 93); *ʾīṯ*, "there is"; *lẹ̄ṯ*, "there is not", etc. In addition we occasionally find the plural ending *-ẹ́*, the 1st sing. perfect of III*ī* verbs with *-ẹ̄ṯí/-īṯí*, the purely etymological writing of ע (טעון/טוען *ṭūn*, "burden", סעורן/סוערן *sūrắn*, "affliction": Dalman 144, 174; תעישוק *tẹ̄šọ́q*, "you oppress": Lev 19:13 etc.) and the south-eastern Aramaic formation of the infinitives of the derived stems in *ọ̄-ẹ́*. From this arose a strictly regularized artificial language, which also indicates the official character of this text. Babylonian Targumic and Babylonian Documentary Aramaic (↗ 25) were imitated in the so-called Nedarim dialect of the Babylonian Talmud (appearing in some late tractates, especially Nedarim; ↗ 45) [16] and in the legal reports of

---

Masoreten des Westens II, Stuttgart 1930, reprint 1967, 63–65. Dalman; E. Brederek, *Konkordanz zum Targum Onqelos*, Gießen 1906; C. J. Kasowski, *Thesaurus Aquilae versionis. Concordantiae verborum quae in Aquilae versione Pentateuchi reperiuntur*, Jerusalem 1940; J. B. van Zijl, *A Concordance to the Targum of Isaiah*, Missoula 1979; J. Levy, *Chaldäisches Wörterbuch über die Targumim* (↗ 8); G. Dalman, *Aramäisch-Neuhebräisches Handwörterbuch* (↗ 8); Kaufman (↗ 8) 161 f.; P. Churgin, *Targum Jonathan to the Prophets*, New Haven 1927, reprints 1980, 1983; A. Tal, *The Language of the Targum of the Former Prophets and its Position within the Aramaic Dialects*, Tel Aviv 1975 (Hebrew); G. E. Weil, "La Massorah", *REJ* 131 (1972) 41–62. The pointing of the Babylonian Targum, established in the 10th cent. B.C., is based on the pronunciation of south-eastern Middle Aramaic (↗ 45).

[16] Dalman 25; Strack-Stemberger 189 f.; S. F. Rybak, *The Aramaic Dialect of Nedarim*, diss. New York 1980. Although the Nedarim dialect and the official language of

the Geonim, the heads of the Jewish academies of Sura and Pumbeditha in northern Babylonia (7th–11th cent. A. D.).[17]

Galilean Targumic, the language of the Galilean Targum,[18] is, like Babylonian Targumic, a mixture of Hasmonaean, in which the original Targum was composed – it reached Galilee from Judaea

---

the Geonim resemble very much Jewish Old Babylonian Aramaic, especially that of the (intentionally archaic) magic bowls (↗ 33 + n. 40), because of the mutual influence of the Jewish written languages of Babylonia, in reality they originate in Post-Achaemenid Imperial Aramaic known from Babylonian Targumic and Babylonian Documentary Aramaic, as especially the emphatic state masc. plur. *-ayyā́* shows.

[17] Dalman 27; I. N. Epstein, *Jahrbuch der Jüdisch-Literarischen Gesellschaft* 9 (1911), 214–304; Strack-Stemberger 21 f., 207 f.

[18] E. G. Clarke, *Targum Pseudo-Jonathan of the Pentateuch. Text and Concordance*, Hoboken/New Jersey 1984 (Jerushalmi I; to Gen-Deut; copied in the 16th cent. A. D.; cf. A. Shinan, *JJS* 36 [1985], 72–87); A. Díez-Macho, *Neophyti I. Targum palestinense*, 6 vols., Madrid 1968–1979 (to Gen-Deut; with many marginal and interlinear variants; copied 1504); M. L. Klein, *The Fragment-Targums of the Pentateuch*, 2 vols., Rome 1980; *Biblia Polyglotta Matritensia*, Series IV: *Targum Palaestinense in Pentateuchum*, ed. A. Díez Macho, 5 vols., Madrid 1977–1985 (Synopsis of all Galilean Targums); R. Le Déaut, *Targum du Pentateuque. Traduction des deux recensions palestiniennes complètes*, 5 vols., Paris 1978–1981; P. de Lagarde, *Prophetae chaldaice*, Leipzig 1872, reprint 1967, VI–XLII, + W. Bacher, *ZDMG* 28 (1874), 1–72 (Fragments of Josh, Judg, 1–2 Sam, 1–2 Kings, Is, Jer, Amos, Jon, Zech); A. Díez Macho, *Estudios bíblicos* 15 (1956), 287–295 (Jos 5:5–6:1); *Biblica* 39 (1958), 198–205 (Ezek 37:1–14); P. de Lagarde, *Hagiographa chaldaice*, Leipzig 1873, reprint 1967; L. Díez Merino, *Targum de Salmos*, Madrid 1982, *Targum de Job*, *Targum de Proverbios*, 1984; A. Sperber, *The Bible in Aramaic*, Vol. IV A, Leiden 1968 (Megillot, Chron); M. J. Mulder, *De Targum op het Hooglied*, Amsterdam 1975, + L. Díez Merino, *Anuario de Filología* 7 (1981), 237–284 (Ms. Ebr. Vat. Urb. 1); E. Levine, *The Aramaic Version of Ruth*, Rome 1973, *Lamentations*, New York 1976, *Qohelet*, New York 1978; A. van der Heide, *The Yemenite Tradition of the Targum of Lamentations. Critical Text and Analysis of the Variant Readings*, Leiden 1981; B. Grossfeld, *The First Targum to Esther*, New York 1983; R. Le Déaut and J. Robert, *Targum des Chroniques*, 2 vols., Rome 1971; M. Ginsburger, *Das Fragmententhargum*, Berlin 1899, reprint 1969, 91–122, and M. Goshen-Gottstein, *Fragments of Lost Targumim* I, Ramat-Gan 1983 (citations); in addition there are a few Aramaic Piyyutim (→ 331) inserted into the reading of the Targum. B. B. Levy, *The Language of Neophyti 1*, diss. New York 1974; D. M. Golomb, *A Grammar of Targum Neofiti*, Chico 1985; S. Lund and J. A. Foster, *Variant Versions of Targumic Traditions within Codex Neofiti* 1, Missoula 1977, with C. Meehan, *JSJ* 9 (1978), 97–104 (the basic text of Neofiti 1 is not unified; its marginal variants are close to Cairo Geniza E or Jerushalmi I); A. Tal, "Ms. Neophyti 1", *IOS* 4 (1974), 31–43 (many scribal errors, strong Babylonian influence). Dalman 27–35; the dictionaries of J. Levy, (↗ 8), G. Dalman (↗ 8) and M. Sokoloff (↗ 49 n.); Kaufman (↗ 8) 162 f.; B. Grossfeld, *Concordance of the First Targum to the Book of Esther*, Chico 1984.

(especially in connection with the Second Jewish Revolt of 132–135 A. D.) –, and the written language of Galilee (↗ 47) which likewise used the "square" script. The Galilean Targum is completely preserved for Gen-Deut and Ps, Job, Song, Ruth, Lam, Eccles, Esther and 1–2 Chron. However, since, despite all its undoubted importance, it did not have any official status (so that its text circulated in a variety of forms and was never definitively fixed), Galilean Targumic, though an artificial language, is not so strictly regulated as Babylonian Targumic.[19] After the Babylonian Targum and Talmud had become authoritative also in Palestine in the 11th cent. A. D. – since 637 A. D. Babylonia (previously Persian) and Palestine (previously Byzantine) had been united under the Caliphate – they exercised considerable influence on the Galilean Targum. Hence Galilean Targumic is preserved in a pure form only in a few fragments from the Cairo Geniza, fragments which were written before 1100 A. D.[20] Non-Galilean features in these texts are: the writing of etymological ʾ (in forms of ראש, "head", בא(י)ר, "well", סנא, "enemy", אכל, "eat", אמר, "say", ברא, "create", קרא, "cry"), of *n* (in אנתה, "wife", לא כל מנדעם, "nothing") and of *ś* (always in עשר, "ten", and derivatives and occasionally otherwise); א in the expression of the emphatic state (increasing) and to express *-ā-* (rarely); -ʾʾ- (instead of shifting to *-yy-*); 2nd

---

[19] Such artificial forms of Aramaic were produced only by communities which already used an artificial pronunciation of Hebrew and Biblical Aramaic, i. e. a composite pronunciation from different periods (→ 123 n. 1). Hence the reason for the preservation of older linguistic elements – of which only the common forms survive as a rule – and the persistence of the consequent mixture lies in the liturgical character of these texts (→ 273). Later additions were written in the same language (→ 331). Both Babylonian Targumic (ending of the emphatic state *-ā́* written with א) and Galilean Targumic (ש for **ś*, נ for **n*) still show that their basis had been Hasmonaean and not Old Judaean. Biblical Aramaic seems only to have affected seriously the pointing of the Targums. All Jewish attempts at pointing try to reconstruct an earlier pronunciation.

[20] M. L. Klein, *Genizah Manuscripts of Palestinian Targum to the Pentateuch*, Cincinnati 1986; S. E. Fassberg, *A Grammar of the Palestinian Targum Fragments from the Cairo Genizah*, Cambridge/Mass. 1986 (fragments A–L: 8th–13th cent. A. D.). The oldest and purest fragments are A and E. Under half was subsequently pointed using Palestinian or Tiberian signs with a mixture of Biblical pronunciation, genuine Galilean pronunciation and mistaken forms. The doublets show the considerable divergences of the individual manuscripts (a parallel to the pre-Christian development of several text forms of the Hebrew Old Testament in Palestine). The additions which have no Hebrew original are more Galilean.

sing. masc. and 3rd sing. fem. suffixes on plural nouns which have not merged with the corresponding suffixes on singular nouns, which contain *a* (mostly: → 153); די, „which; that" (as well as ד); the artificial (→ 116 + n. 1) ending (prompted by the corresponding Galilean *-áy* [→ 149]) of the absolute masc. plur. from III*ī* nouns, of the 2nd fem. sing. imperfect of III*ī* verbs and of the dual, *-áyən*, which comes from the Hebraizing pronunciation of Biblical Aramaic and is also always applied to *ʿáyən*, "eye", and *hāʾẹlláyən* (< *-ẹ́n* < *-ẹ̄n*), "these"; the absolute masc. plur. *-āʾín* (sometimes) and emphatic masc. plur. *-āʾẹ́* (mostly) of the gentilic-type adjective in *-áy* instead of Galilean *-āyín*, *-āyẹ́* (↗ 21, → 453); the afformatives of the 3rd masc. plur. perfect and masc. plur. imperative *-ū* (instead of Galilean *-ún*: ↗ 39; though in III*ī* verbs Galilean *-ọ́n*) and of the fem. sing. imperative *-ī* (instead of Galilean *-ín*); the preformative of the 1st sing. imperfect ʾ- (more frequently than Galilean *n-*: ↗ 39, → 152); the jussive; the qal infinitive without the vowel of the imperfect (also in verbs II*ū*); the infinitive of the derived stems without *m-* (only in the construct) and with *-ūṯ* before suffixes (always); the 1st sing. perfect of the derived stems from III*ī* roots not in *-iyẹ́ṯ*; the placing of demonstratives after the noun (almost always); מאה, "hundred" (Gen 7:11E), after numbers instead of Galilean מאו(ו)ן plur. (Gen 7:6E; cf. 32:15C; ↗ 39); the participle as historic present (↗ 15) in ע(א)ני ואמר, "he began and said" (Gen 4:8,8B; 29:22E); the imperfect (of course 1st sing. only ʾ-) as present and future in main clause (instead of participle; usually); accusative particle ית before nouns and the almost complete replacement of the object suffixes by ית with suffixes; Hebrew-Aramaic mixed-forms (cohortative etc.); numerous particular words (cf. Dalman 44–51) like ארום, "that; because; if", ה(א), the interrogative particle (instead of המ), חזי, "see" (instead of חמי), כען, "now" (instead of כדון), the independent personal pronouns אנון, א(י)נין, "they", and the question words אן, "where?", and אידא, אילין, "which?", still beginning with ʾ instead of shifting to *h*; and after the 7th cent. A. D. final stress (→ 146) and long vowels in closed final syllables. In addition all Targums tend to Hebraize, even in the additional sections which have no Hebrew original. Greek words decrease.

Babylonian Documentary Aramaic is used from the 3rd cent. A. D. onwards (↗ 22; 33 n. 39) for Babylonian Jewish private documents and eventually from the 12th cent. A. D. onwards for all Jewish private documents in Aramaic.[21] The oldest examples are marriage contracts and bills of divorce from the Cairo Geniza written in the 11th cent. A.D. in Egypt and citations in private Galilean documents (↗ 49 n.58). This written language is based, like Babylonian and Galilean Targumic, on Hasmonaean, in which private Jewish documents were being composed even after 37 B.C. (demonstrably until at least 135 A.D.; ↗ 20). These Hasmonaean formularies remained in use in Babylonia almost unaltered, while in Palestine they were superseded by Galilean (↗ 49). As the Cairo Geniza documents especially show, Babylonian Documentary Aramaic stands much closer to Hasmonaean than Babylonian Targumic: אנתי, "you" fem. sing.; יכי, „your" fem. sing.; די, „which"; א(י)נתתי, "my wife"; עשר, "ten". Jewish Old Babylonian features are especially: דנן and הדין, "this"; בת, "daughter", construct; 1st sing. perfect of III*ī* verbs in *-ẹ̄ṯī́/-īṯī́*; 3rd person imperfect of הוי, "to be", *yẹ-*; הנעילת, "she brought in" (hafʿel of *ʿll*); נדוניא, "dowry". The 2nd fem. sing. imperfect of III*ī* verbs in (י)יין *-yī́n* is artificial.

Nabataean is the written language of the Arab kingdom of Petra (*Raqm*), which had its origins c. 400 B.C., became a kingdom c. 200 B.C. and was annexed to the Roman Empire as the Provincia Arabia in 106 A.D. It embraced the Sinai Peninsula, the area east of the Jordan (cf. 2 Cor 11:32) and north-western Arabia and owed its prosperity above all to the caravan trade. The Nabataeans opted for Aramaic, although Old North Arabic was demonstrably used for writing even from the 6th century B.C. (→ 86 + n.1). Nabataean is found in almost 1000 tomb and votive inscriptions, all more or less similar in form, principally from the areas of Petra, Bosra and Hegra from about 170 B.C. (Ḫalaṣa in Southern Palestine: Cantineau II, 43f.) to 356 A.D. (south-west of Teima in the Arabian desert: Bulletin 1971, 125), though mostly from the 1st century A.D., and in more than 3000 short commemorative inscriptions from the south of the Sinai Peninsula dated 150–267 A.D.[22] There are in addition nine private con-

---

[21] On the formularies: G. Dalman, *Aramäische Dialektproben*, 2nd ed., Leipzig 1927, reprint 1960, 4f.; → 324. Private documents from the Cairo Geniza: S. Assaf, *Tarbiz* 9 (1937/38), 30–34.

[22] The inscriptions published to 1907 are collected in *CIS* 157–3233, almost all those thereafter to 1919 in *RES* I–IV; those published to 1938 have been listed by F. Rosenthal (↗ 8) 299; thereafter: C.H. Kraeling, *Gerasa*, New Haven 1938, 371–373; Aimé-Giron (↗ 16 n.) 123; E. Littmann, *BSOAS* 15 (1953), 1–28; 16 (1954), 211–246;

tracts and a fragment from the caves beside the Dead Sea from around 100 A.D. (→319f.). A Nabataean letter is attested for as early as 312 B.C. (Cantineau, I, 11, cf. Bulletin 1970, 54). The Nabataean texts are easy to recognize because of their characteristic script, a cursive hand out of which the modern Arabic script emerged. If one disregards the sound change *l/n* coming from colloquial Arabic (אלוש, צנם, the name מנכו) and about 25 Arabic words, Nabataean stands nearer to Achaemenid Imperial Aramaic than does Hasmonaean. From the 3rd cent. A.D. onwards the Arabic words and forms greatly increase and in the 4th cent. A.D. Nabataean finally merges, without a break, into Arabic: the en-Nemāra inscription (from south of Damascus; 328 A.D.)[23] contains the single Aramaic word *bàr*, "son".

Palmyrene is found, apart from a single line on a receipt from Dura-Europos,[24] exclusively in inscriptions from 44 B.C. to 274 A.D. (in so far as they are dated), in the main from the 2nd and 3rd cent. A.D. They come predominantly from the ancient commercial centre of Palmyra (*Tadmọ́r*) and are written for the most part in a rounded ornamental script, though from the second half of the 1st cent. A.D. onwards also sometimes in a cursive script similar to Syriac Estrangela. The most important text is the Greek-Palmyrene taxation tariff of 18th April 137 A.D.; besides this there are over 1000 honorary, votive and tomb inscriptions.[25] Palmyrene is the dialect of Eastern

---

R. Savignac and J. Starcky, *RB* 64 (1957), 196–217; J.T. Milik, *Syria* 35 (1958), 227–251; Bulletin under "Nabatéen"; J.T. Milik and J. Starcky, in: *CIS* 3234ff.; Schürer I 726–744/574–586; J. Cantineau, *Le Nabatéen. Grammaire, choix de textes, lexique*, 2 vols., Paris 1930, 1932, reprint 1978; *DISO*: "Nab."; M. Lindner (ed.), *Petra und das Königreich der Nabatäer*, 4th ed., Munich 1983; A. Negev, "The Nabataeans and the Provincia Arabia", in: *Aufstieg und Niedergang der römischen Welt II* 8, Berlin 1977, 520–686; G.W. Bowersock, *Roman Arabia*, Cambridge/Mass. 1983; R. Wenning, *Die Nabatäer. Denkmäler und Geschichte*, Göttingen 1986. The Imperial Aramaic writing of Arabic names (from 400 B.C.), which has been retained in Hebrew and Middle Aramaic, is the starting point of Arabic orthography. This is phonetic except for the false etymology in the writing of every *s* (not only *s* < *š*) with ש (→ 101 n. end), which lead in Arabic to the loss of ס, cf. W. Diem, *Orientalia* 48 (1979), 207–257; 49 (1980), 67–106; 50 (1981), 332–383; 52 (1983), 357–404. But י stands only for *-ā* < *-ay(u/a)*, cf. Teima 24,3 (c. 400 B.C.) the personal name העלי *Háʿlay* "Highest".

[23] *ESE* 2, 34–36; Cantineau II 49f.; J.A. Bellamy, *JAOS* 105 (1985), 31–48.

[24] H. Ingholt, in: *The Excavations at Dura-Europos, Final Report V 1*, New York 1959, 141f., no. 27d, 3.

[25] The inscriptions published to 1926 are collected in *CIS* 3901–4624, while independently of this those found in Palmyra are collected in the *Inventaire des inscriptions*

Aramaic spoken in Palmyra (↗ 31). However, the inscriptions have still retained one Imperial Aramaic form, namely the replacing of the 3rd fem. plural of the perfect with the masculine (Tariff I:5 אסקו והוו), and several Imperial Aramaic orthographic features. These show that previously Imperial Aramaic was written in Palmyra and that the continuity of Aramaic here – by contrast with the rest of the north-eastern Aramaic area (↗ 31) – had never been interrupted by Greek, although this played an important role as the official language of the Seleucids and the eastern half of the Roman Empire, as is proved by the numerous Greek-Palmyrene bilinguals in Palmyra. The Imperial Aramaic orthographic features (partly preserved also in the rest of north-eastern Aramaic) are: אנת (= Syriac) *'aṯ* (→ 121), "you" (masc. sing.); אנתתה (= Syriac, East Mesopotamian) *'attẹh,* "his wife" (otherwise always אתתה); די (→ 549) *da,* "which; that" (as well as ד); ברת (= Syriac, East Mesopotamian, Mandaic) *bàṯ* (only in construct), "daughter" (as well as בת); haf'el instead of af'el (→ 148); particularly, however, the ending of the emphatic masc. plur. *-ẹ̄* (→ 98) with יא, which interchanges with the less common ending א even in the Tax Tariff – so in I:10 in the divine name רב אסירא Ραβ ασειρη *Ràḇ 'asīrẹ̄,* "lord of the captives (souls)" – and was clearly retained because of its unequivocal meaning.[26] Imperial Aramaic merged into Eastern Aramaic in Palmyra probably in the course of the 2nd cent. B.C. (↗ 31). As the high proportion of Arab names shows, most of the inhabitants of Palmyra were Arabs. This explains the Arabic influence in Palmyrene.

Arsacid is the official language of the Parthian Empire (247 B.C. to 224 A.D.).[27] Script, orthography and style agree sometimes almost

de Palmyre, begun by J. Cantineau, 1930ff.; Bulletin under "Palmyrénien"; J. T. Milik, *Dédicaces faites par des dieux (Palmyre, Hatra, Tyr) et de thiases sémitiques à l'époque romaine,* Paris 1972; J. Cantineau, *Grammaire du Palmyrénien épigraphique,* Cairo 1935; R. Rosenthal, *Die Sprache der palmyrenischen Inschriften,* Leipzig 1936; *DISO*: "Palm."; J. K. Stark, *Personal Names in Palmyrene Inscriptions,* Oxford 1971; H. J. W. Drijvers, "Hatra [803–837], Palmyra [837–863] and Edessa [863–896]. Die Städte der syrisch-mesopotamischen Wüste in politischer, kulturgeschichtlicher und religionsgeschichtlicher Beleuchtung", in: *Aufstieg und Niedergang der römischen Welt II* 8, Berlin 1977, 799–906; id., *The Religion of Palmyra,* Leiden 1976; J. Teixidor, *The Pantheon of Palmyra,* Leiden 1979; id., "Palmyre et son commerce d'Auguste à Caracalla", *Semitica* 34 (1984), 1–127.

[26] Also the etymological writing of the ittaf. of עלל in the Tariff is artificial (→ 469).

[27] Brick inscription from Uruk (c. 200 B.C.): O. Krückmann, in: *7. vorläufiger Bericht über die ... in Uruk-Warka unternommenen Ausgrabungen,* Berlin 1936, 36.

completely with Achaemenid Imperial Aramaic. However, from the beginning there are also later letter-forms, more frequent expression in writing of medial vowels (especially *ā* and *ẹ*) and growing influ-

---

9 boundary-stones from Armenia (so far dated 180 B.C.): Bulletin 1972, 142; 1973, 171.

About 2500 ostraca from Nisa in Parthia with almost identical details on the content of storage vessels (2nd–1st cent. B.C.) Bulletin 1973, 161–169.

9 relief inscriptions from Arebsun in Cappadocia (c. 100 B.C.: → 120): *ESE* 1, 59–74, 319–326; *RES* 1785 (E = *KAI* 264).

Inscription from Farasa in Cappadocia (+ Greek; around birth of Christ): *ESE* 3, 66f.; *RES* 966; *KAI* 265; E. Lipiński (↗ 13 n.7) 173–184.

Bill of sale from Awroman in Media (53 A.D.): F. Altheim and R. Stiehl, *Geschichte Mittelasiens im Altertum*, Berlin 1970, 483–491.

Inscription 1 from Armazi in Georgia (second half of 1st cent. A.D.): F. Altheim and R. Stiehl, *Die aramäische Sprache unter den Achaimeniden*, Frankfurt 1963, 243–261.

Inscription 2 from Armazi in Georgia (+ Greek; first half of 2nd cent. A.D.): *KAI* 276 + R. Degen, *ZDMG* 121 (1971), 138.

Silver dish from Sissian in Armenia (2nd cent. A.D.): Bulletin 1973, 172.

Inscription from Garni in Armenia (c. 200 A.D.; *r* indicated by point placed over it): J. Naveh, *IOS* 2 (1972), 297f.

6 relief inscriptions from Tang-i Sarvak in Elymais (2nd cent. A.D.): W. B. Henning, *Asia Major* 2 (1952), 151–178; S. Shaked, *BSOAS* 27 (1964), 287–290. R. Macuch, in: F. Altheim and R. Stiehl, *Die Araber in der alten Welt II*, Berlin 1965, 139–158; id., *Theologische Literaturzeitung* 90 (1965), 656f.

5 relief inscriptions from Šimbar in Elymais (2nd cent. A.D.): A. D. H. Bivar and S. Shaked, *BSOAS* 27 (1964), 265–281; R. Macuch, *Theologische Literaturzeitung* 90 (1965), 657–660; F. Altheim and R. Stiehl, *Die Araber in der alten Welt III*, Berlin 1966, 66–73; Bulletin 1967, 70.

Numerous inscriptions in ink from Šimbar in Elymais (1st–3rd cent. A.D.): A. D. H. Bivar and S. Shaked, *BSOAS* 27 (1964), 281–287.

Stone inscription from Bard-ē Nešande in Persia (beginning of 3rd cent. A.D.): F. Altheim and R. Stiehl, *Die Araber in der alten Welt V 1*, Berlin 1968, 77f.

Letter (2nd–3rd cent. A.D.): W. B. Henning, in: *The Excavations at Dura-Europos, Final Report V 1*, New Haven 1959, 414f., no. 153; F. Altheim and R. Stiehl, *Die aramäische Sprache unter den Achaimeniden*, 64–73.

Relief inscription from Susa (215 A.D.): F. Altheim and R. Stiehl, *Supplementum Aramaicum*, Baden-Baden 1957, 98–100; id., *Die aramäische Sprache unter den Achaimeniden*, 47f.

Stone inscription from northern Persia (not closely datable): *CIS* 111.

Coins (2nd cent. B.C.–3rd cent. A.D.): G. Le Rider, *Suse sous les Séleucides et les Parthes*, Paris 1965; F. Altheim and R. Stiehl, *Die aramäische Sprache unter den Achaimeniden*, 51–55, 284, 290f., 306.

Vocabulary is provided by *DISO*: "Aram. Emp."; F. Altheim and R. Stiehl, *Die aramäische Sprache unter den Achaimeniden*, 262–277.

ence from south-eastern Aramaic (*ḥ* > *h*, ʿ > ʾ, sometimes *h* > ʾ), Georgian (masc. = fem.) and Persian. From the 1st cent. A.D. onwards local variant forms of Arsacid developed, corresponding to the loose structure of the Parthian Empire. When the Sassanids (224–642 A.D.) brought in Middle Persian (Pahlavi) as the official language at the beginning of their rule, they took over the script from Arsacid and used many words as logograms.[28] However, the Aramaean population of Babylonia turned their south-eastern Aramaic colloquial into a written language, so that the Mandaeans preserved some Arsacid orthographic features (ז for **ḏ*, ק for **ḡ*, ע for *ʿ), which they had adopted together with the Arsacid script after their migration into Southern Babylonia, since they lacked a written form of language of their own[29] (↗ 46). The Babylonian Jews, on the other hand, formed a special written language of their own under the influence of Jewish Old Palestinian (↗ 33).

Old Eastern Aramaic

The Old Eastern Aramaic spoken dialects of Mesopotamia, Babylonia and the area east of the Tigris are attested as early as the 9th–3rd cent. B.C. in numerous words[30] and names[31] appearing in Akka-

---

[28] More than 600 logograms survive: F. Altheim and R. Stiehl, *Die aramäische Sprache unter den Achaimeniden*, 278–308; E. Y. Kutscher, Aramaic (↗ 8) 393–399; *DISO*: "Paik., Phrah., Sogd."; e.g. מלכא *šāh*, "king".

[29] Nöldeke-Schall, *Mandäische Grammatik*, 6, 43 f., 72 f.; F. Rosenthal (↗ 8) 228, 230, 235; Bulletin 1971, 1.

[30] W. v. Soden, "Aramäische Wörter in neuassyrischen und neu- und spätbabylonischen Texten", *Orientalia* 35 (1966), 1–20; 37 (1968), 261–271; 46 (1977), 183–197; id., *Akkadisches Handwörterbuch*, Wiesbaden 1965–1981 ("*AHw*"); *The Assyrian Dictionary of the Oriental Institute of the University of Chicago*, 1956 ff. ("*CAD*").

[31] K. L. Tallqvist, *Assyrian Personal Names*, Helsingfors 1914, reprint 1966 ("*APN*"); R. Zadok, *On West Semites in Babylonia during the Chaldean and Achaemenian Periods. An Onomastic Study*, 2nd. ed., Jerusalem 1978 (the Aramaic and Arabic names from neo-Assyrian and neo- and late Babylonian cuneiform texts; "*WSB*"); id., *The Jews in Babylonia during the Chaldean and Achaemenian Periods according to the Babylonian Sources*, Haifa 1979 ("*JCAB*"); Bulletin 1979, 40; S. Parpola, *Neo-Assyrian Toponyms*, Neukirchen 1970 ("*NAT*"). Cf. J. A. Brinkman, *A Political History of Post-Kassite Babylon (1158–722 B.C.)*, Rome 1968; M. Dietrich, *Die Aramäer Südbabyloniens in der Sargonidenzeit (700–648 v. Chr.)*, Neukirchen 1970, with J. A. Brinkman, *Orientalia* 46 (1977), 304–325; J. Eph'al, "The Western Minorities in Babylonia in the 6th–5th Centuries B.C. Maintenance and Cohesion", *Orientalia* 47 (1978), 74–90; B. Oded, *Mass*

dian cuneiform texts. The correspondence of the company of Muraššu and Sons of Nippur (455–403 B.C.)[32] in particular contains many Aramaic (including also Jewish) personal names. The most important cuneiform evidence, however, is the Uruk text, a 43-line tablet from Uruk in Babylonia containing two partly matching Aramaic magic texts (c. 150 B.C.).[33] Further, northern Old Eastern Aramaic is known indirectly from the north-eastern Aramaic impact on the Gozan inscription, the Hermopolis papyri and Ahiqar (↗ 15 n.10; → 98; 103; 150) and late southern Old Eastern Aramaic from the south-eastern Aramaic impact on Arsacid (↗ 29f.).

The northern Old Eastern dialects of Aramaic became written languages in the 2nd cent. B.C. in the context of the Semitic reaction against Hellenism. So only in Palmyra did Imperial Aramaic merge without a break into Eastern Aramaic (↗ 28; as later, in southern Babylonia, Arsacid merged into Mandaic; ↗ 30), while Old Syriac and East Mesopotamian obviously came directly from the local dialects, since here the continuity of written Aramaic had been interrupted by Greek by the end of the 4th cent. B.C. The script and some orthographic conventions (↗ 28) were thus taken over from Arsacid. Old Syriac, the official language of the kingdom of Osrhoene, founded by an Arab dynasty in Edessa in 132 B.C. and surviving until 242 A.D., is known from about 80 inscriptions (mostly burial, cultic and commemorative) of the 1st–3rd cent. A.D. (from 6 A.D.) and from a deed of sale of 243 A.D. It is characterized by an unusually firm orthography. It differs from the later Middle Syriac (↗ 43) in certain conspicuous ways (especially: still no diacritics on *d/r*, the plural etc.; ש for *ś;

Deportations and Deportees in the Neo-Assyrian Empire, Wiesbaden 1979; P.Garelli, "Importance et rôle des Araméens dans l'administration de l'empire assyrien", in: H.-J.Nissen and J.Renger (eds.), *Mesopotamien und seine Nachbarn,* Berlin 1982, 437–447; H.Tadmor, "The Aramaization of Assyria", ibid. 449–470.

32 M.D.Coogan, *West Semitic Personal Names in the Murašū Documents,* Missoula 1976 ("*Muraššu*") with R.Zadok, *BASOR* 231 (1978), 73–78; M.W.Stolper, "Yahwistic Personal Names in the Murašū Texts", *BASOR* 222 (1976), 25–28; several names are Hebrew. Dating according to: R.A.Parker and W.H.Dubberstein, *Babylonian Chronology 626 B.C.–A.D. 75,* 3rd ed., Providence 1969.

33 C.H.Gordon, *Archiv für Orientforschung* 12 (1938), 105–117; B.Landsberger, ibid., 247–257; C.H.Gordon, *Orientalia* 9 (1940), 29–38; A.Dupont-Sommer, *RA* 39 (1942/44), 35–62; *DISO*: "Warka"; according to J.J.A. van Dijk (letter of 6/2/1969) c. 150 B.C. The careful transcription and fixed orthography indicate a scribal school. The syntax is archaic, though the pronunciation is clearly that of its own time.

3rd person imperfect preformative *y*-). Although there was a Christian church in Edessa as early as 201 A.D. – it was destroyed in the famous flood – all the Old Syriac inscriptions are pagan.[34] East Mesopotamian, which was used as a written language on both sides of the upper Tigris, is preserved in several hundred inscriptions from Hatra (including surrounding area; present dating 89–238 A. D.), which, after a small beginning as a stopping-off place for caravans, was a Parthian kingdom from about 165 A.D. until its capture by the Sassanids in 240/241 A.D.,[35] Assur (200–228 A.D.)[36] and Sari and Hassankef in the Ṭur-ʿAbdin (235/6 and 195 A.D.).[37] It is also preserved in the older, upper inscription on the sarcophagus of Queen Helena of Adiabene, a convert to Judaism, found in Jersualem (→ 342f.; 40–50 A.D.). East Mesopotamian differs from Syriac especially in the 3rd person imperfect preformative *l*- (→ 98) and the systematic change *aw* > *ọ̄* and *ay* > *ẹ̄* (→ 117). Also Tatian, who came from Assyria, must have used East Mesopotamian for the composition of his Diatessaron – whether he had brought home from Rome in 172 A.D. only the Greek *Vorlage* or (which is less likely) the

---

[34] H.J.W. Drijvers, *Old-Syriac (Edessean) Inscriptions. Ed. with an Introduction, Indices and a Glossary*, Leiden 1972, + *BSOAS* 36 (1973), 1–14, + *Muséon* 95 (1982), 167–189, with R. Degen, *BiOr* 31 (1974), 293–296, + *NESE* 2, 105–109, J. Naveh, *BASOR* 216 (1974), 10f.; cf. K. Beyer, *ZDMG* 116 (1966), 242–248; Bulletin under "Syriaque"; H.J.W. Drijvers (↗ 28 n.). In addition the archival report of the flood in Edessa in November 201 A.D., which was written in 206–212 A.D., was of course composed in Old Syriac, though in its present form, preserved in the Edessene Chronicle (of c. 540 A.D.), ed. L. Hallier, Leipzig 1892, 145–147 (= C. Brockelmann, *Syrische Grammatik*, 6th ed., Leipzig 1951, 21*–23*; F. Rosenthal [ed.], *An Aramaic Handbook*, Wiesbaden 1967, II/1, 23–25), it is completely converted into Middle Syriac (↗ 43, → 156).

[35] W. Andrae, *Hatra I*, Leipzig 1908, reprint 1984, 28f,. and *Hatra II*, 1912, reprint 1975, 161–164; F. Vattioni, *Le iscrizioni di Ḥatra*, Naples 1981 (356 inscriptions) + J. B. Segal, *JJS* 33 (1982), 109–115 (2 inscriptions); W. Al-Salihi, *Iraq* 45 (1983), 140–145 (7); J. Kh. Ibrahim, *New Evidence for Settlement in the Jazirah in the Pre-Islamic Period*, diss. London 1981 (22 from Hatra, 5 from Jaddalah); S. Abbadi, *Die Personennamen der Inschriften aus Hatra*, Hildesheim 1983; Bulletin under "Hatréen"; *DISO*: "Hatra"; J.T. Milik (↗ 28 n.), especially 323–408; H.J.W. Drijvers (↗ ibid.).

[36] Mostly memorial inscriptions: P. Jensen, *Sitzungsberichte der preußischen Akademie der Wissenschaften* 1919 II, 1042–1051; id., *Mitteilungen der Deutschen Orientgesellschaft* 60 (1920), 1–47; W. Andrae and H. Lenzen, *Die Partherstadt Assur*, Leipzig 1933, 105–111 (105f.: 2 inscriptions at least about a century older) + plates 33, 36, 39, 57, 59; J. Naveh, *IOS* 2 (1972), 293–304; *DISO*: "Hatra".

[37] F. Vattioni (↗ 32 n.35) 107f.; B. Aggoula, *Semitica* 32 (1982), 101–109.

finished Aramaic work – since he despised all things Greek, was considered by the Greek church heretical and would have reached in Greek only a thin upper-crust of his compatriots.[38]

On the other hand southern Old Eastern Aramaic was used only by the Jews as a written language: they created for themselves in c. 70 A.D. (↗ 37 n.47; before 37 B.C. they would have taken over Hasmonaean), in imitation of Jewish Old Palestinian (↗ 35: square script; ה for the emphatic ending *-ā́*; ס for **ś*), Jewish Old Babylonian Aramaic, which, however, came increasingly under the influence of Biblical Aramaic and Babylonian Targumic (א instead of ה for *-ā́*; again ש for **ś*). It is represented by a private contract (200 A.D.)[39] from Dura-Europos, numerous Jewish magic bowls from Babylonia (4th–6th cent. A.D.), into which, however, a later element has penetrated from the scribes (sound changes; 3rd person imperfect preformative *n-*; etc.),[40] and the south-eastern Aramaic layer of Babylonian Targumic (↗ 22). Jews also sometimes wrote northern Old Eastern Aramaic in square script, as three Jewish Old Syriac tomb inscriptions from the Edessa region show (2nd–3rd cent. A.D.).[41] As

---

[38] A. Vööbus, *Early Versions of the New Testament,* Stockholm 1954, 1–31; B.M. Metzger, *The Early Versions of the New Testament,* Oxford 1977, 10–36; *Biblia Polyglotta Matritensia Series VI. Vetus Evangelium Syrorum et exinde excerptum Diatessaron Tatiani,* ed. I. Ortiz de Urbina, Madrid 1967. The Diatessaron is preserved in Aramaic only in Syriac fragments. ↗ 36 n.46.

[39] J.T. Milik, *Syria* 45 (1968), 97–104; → 110.

[40] These demon-traps (mostly buried upside down under houses, occasionally with a second bowl as a lid) are rarely tops of skulls, mostly bowls of fired clay instead, which carry spiral inscriptions (ח for **ḥ* and **h*). W.H. Rossell, *A Handbook of Aramaic Magical Texts,* Ringwood Borough/New Jersey 1953 (grammar + 30 texts); C.D. Isbell, *Corpus of the Aramaic Incantation Bowls,* Missoula 1975 (72 texts), + *BASOR* 223 (1976), 15–23 (2 texts); A.J. Borisov, *Epigrafika Vostoka* 19 (1969), 3–13; S.A. Kaufman, *JNES* 32 (1973), 170–174 (1; only Hebrew Bible and Targum Jonathan Jer 2,1 f.); M.J. Geller, *BSOAS* 39 (1976), 425–427 (1); C.H. Gordon, in: *Festschrift W.S. LaSor,* Grand Rapids 1978, 231–244 (2); K.A.D. Smelik, *BiOr* 35 (1978), 174–177 (1); F. Franco, *Mesopotamia* 13/14 (1978/79), 233–249 (5); M.J. Geller, in: *Festschrift C.H. Gordon,* New York 1980, 47–60 (4); T. Harviainen, *Studia Orientalia* 51:14 (1981), 3–25 (1); C.H. Gordon, *Orientalia* 53 (1984), 220–241 (2); J. Naveh and S. Shaked, *Amulets and Magic Bowls,* Jerusalem 1985 (11); cf. J.N. Epstein, "Gloses babylo-araméennes", *REJ* 73 (1921), 27–58; 74 (1922), 40–72; J. Neusner, *A History of the Jews in Babylonia V.* Leiden 1970, 217–243 and (by B.A. Levine) 343–375; Bulletin under "Araméen". Some 50 bowls, discovered 1948–1967 by the Chicago Oriental Institute Nippur Expedition, are still unpublished (cf. *Nippur*, vol. 1, Chicago 1967, pls. 164–167).

[41] Frey 1415, 1416, 1418 (הנא "this").

the official language of Dura-Europos (destroyed by the Sassanids in 256 A.D.) was Greek, little is known of the Aramaic of this area (→ 131); for neither the Aramaeans mentioned by name in Greek and Latin texts (→ 113 f., 116), nor the author of the inscription written in Greek letters (before 256 A.D.)[42] need originate from there. Mani (216–276 A.D.), the founder of Manichaeism, could have used any of the eastern dialects for his Aramaic works except Palmyrene, Old Syriac and Jewish Old Babylonian.[43]

Old Western Aramaic

Starting from western Syria, Aramaic gained acceptance throughout Palestine by the 4th cent. B.C.[44] Only Phoenician continued to be

---

[42] → 133: J.T. Milik, *Syria* 44 (1967), 289–306; Bulletin 1970, 85; B. Aggoula, *Semitica* 32 (1982), 110 (i.e.: λα "by" instead of αα); → 114 n. 1. But all the surrounding Aramaic dialects are represented at Dura-Europos: Palmyrene, Old Syriac, East Mesopotamian, Jewish Old Babylonian, Arsacid and even Jewish Middle Palestinian (↗ 53), as well as numerous Aramaic names in Greek and Latin transcription. Cf. *The Excavations at Dura-Europos, Preliminary Report* 1929 ff., *Final Report* 1943 ff.; C. Hopkins–B. Goldman, *The Discovery of Dura-Europos*, New Haven 1979.

[43] F. Rosenthal (↗ 8) 207–211; → 259.

[44] Northern Hebrew was spoken in Palestine until about 500 B.C. and southern Hebrew until about 400 B.C., less long in the Assyrian and Babylonian exile (Old Hebrew: ↗ 9 n. 2). Southern Hebrew is continued in Middle Hebrew, which was used until about 100 A.D. especially by priests, prophets and apocalypticists (Middle Hebrew[1] = Biblical Middle Hebrew: Is 24–27, Joel, Jon, Zech 9–14, late Psalms, Job, Ruth, Esther, Dan, Ezra, Neh, 1–2 Chron, i.e. about a quarter of the Old Testament; Middle Hebrew[2] = post-Biblical Middle Hebrew: Enoch, Judith, Tob, Sir, Mart Is, Jub, I Macc,, Test Neph, Ep Jer, Ps of Sol, Vit Ad, Ass Mos, Ethiopic Enoch 37–71, Zosimus [*JSJ* 9, 68–82], most of the Hebrew writings found in Qumran; and after 70 A.D.: 4 Ezra, Bar, Apoc of Bar [syr.], Test XII Patr, Pseudo-Philo, Paralipomena Jeremiae, Apoc Abrah, Piyyutim in the Middle Ages). Neo-Hebrew (including the artificial language of the Mishna), also an old sacred language, is the academic language of the sages and lawyers (most notable characteristics: ש instead of אשר, של instead of construct, זו "this" fem., Nitpa'el, loss of *waw*- consecutive, restriction of conjunctionless hypotaxis); it is strongly influenced by Aramaic, though it shows also the impact of northern Hebrew, and is first observable in the 3rd cent. B.C. (Biblical Neo-Hebrew: Song, Qo, but influenced by the Middle Hebrew of the copyists). In pure form it appears from the 1st cent. B.C. on in several unpublished texts from Qumran cave 4 (J. Strugnell, cf. e.g. *DJD* 3, 222–227), the Copper Scroll (ibid., 199–302), contracts and letters from the Dead Sea (132–135 A.D.) and inscriptions (Neo-Hebrew[1]) and from the 8th cent. A.D. in the early manuscripts of rabbinic and liturgical texts (Palestinian/Babylonian Neo-Hebrew[2]); by contrast the late manuscripts and printed

spoken until the 1st cent. B.C.[45] Like northern Old Eastern Aramaic, Old Western Aramaic became a language of writing in the 2nd cent. B.C. specifically in the form of Jewish Old Palestinian and Pagan Old Palestinian, both of which arose at the same time in the same area.

Jewish Old Palestinian uses the square script (↗ 20 n. 14; rarely also the old Hebrew script: → 346f.). It appears first in the form of Old East Jordanian and specifically in the oldest Enoch manuscript (c. 170 B.C.; → 227). It is next seen in the form of Old Judaean, to which belong: tomb, ossuary and other inscriptions from Jerusalem, Jericho and the Wadi Suwenit (37 B.C.–70 A.D.; → 6, 339–348), boundary-stones from Gezer (c. 70 A.D.; → 339), ostraca from Masada (66–75 A.D.; → 349), receipts from Qumran (down to 68 A.D.; → 350) and Murabbaʿat (down to 135 A.D.; → 348f.), letters of Simon bar Kosiba (134–135 A.D.; → 350–352), an inscription in Greek script from Beersheba (2nd cent. A.D.; → 353), as well as a few texts preserved in the Talmud: inscriptions on the offering chests in the Temple (9 B.C.; → 360), the calendar of fasts (*Megillath Taʿanith*; 67–70 A.D.; → 354–358), circular letters of Rabban Gamaliel II (c. 100 A.D.; → 359f.), sayings of the scribes (20 B.C.–135 A.D.; → 360–362) and a legendary heavenly message to John Hyrcanus I (→ 360). Old Judaean was also the language in which Josephus had written the first, non-extant, edition of his Jewish War (War 1, 1, 3 τῇ πατρίῳ γλώσσῃ; c. 75 A.D.). Pagan Old Palestinian is known so far only from a short Old East Jordanian building inscription from el-Mal, north-east of the Sea of Galilee (7/6 B.C.; → 406; also as early as c. 200 B.C. from Dan near Her-

books on which most of the modern grammars and dictionaries of Neo-Hebrew are based are closer to Biblical Hebrew (Neo-Hebrew[3]). The official language of the state of Israel (Modern Hebrew, Ivrit) is based on the Neo-Hebrew used in eastern Europe.

[45] Meleager of Gadara (c. 100 B.C.) distinguished Aramaic, Phoenician and Greek (the Phoenician greeting is corrupted: one would expect σαλωμ): A.S.F. Gow and D. L. Page, *The Greek Anthology. Hellenistic Epigrams*, Cambridge 1965, I 217 ἀλλ' εἰ μὲν Σύρος ἐσσί, σαλαμ· εἰ δ'οὖν σύ γε Φοῖνιξ, ναιδιος· εἰ δ' Ἕλλην, χαῖρε. From Plutarch *Sulla* 17,8 θωρ οἱ Φοίνικες τὴν βοῦν καλοῦσι one can hardly conclude that around 100 A.D. Phoenician had been completely pushed out by Aramaic (Aram. *tọ̄r*, "bull"; in Phoenician it would have had to be *šọ̄r* σωρ). Later, Phoenician place-names were Aramaized like Hebrew after 400 B.C., cf. S. Wild (↗ 54 n. 65) 122 *Rāmūṭ* from Phoenician *Rọ̄mūt*, "hills" (ọ̄ < ā and ū < ā can appear in the same word: Plautus *Poenulus* 930 alonuth, "goddesses").

mon? ↗ 17 n.). Its script is close to that of Palmyrene and Syriac, though Palmyrene, Syriac and East Mesopotamian, unlike Pagan Old Palestinian, almost always use א for *-ā́*. It seems that a Christian Old Palestinian developed from the Pagan version; it is only indirectly attested[46] and has no connection with the later Christian Palestinian (↗ 51). Old Palestinian is clearly contrasted with Imperial Aramaic (↗ 21), though Jewish Palestinian fell under the influence of Hasmonaean and Biblical Aramaic (they have the square script in common) and vice versa (↗ 19, 21). One may note that later forms have penetrated the Old Judaean texts transmitted in the Talmud, while on the other hand עשר, "ten", and its derivatives are again written with שׂ as in Galilean Targumic (↗ 24) and sometimes also in Middle Judaean (↗ 49). Since Jewish Old Palestinian already has ס for **ś* (*ś* > *s* in the course of the 2nd cent. B.C.: → 103), but still indicates unaccented

[46] The anonymous Old Syriac translation of the Gospels (Vetus Syra) seems to have its origin here. Since the canon of the four Gospels (which contradicts the claim to exclusiveness of the individual Gospels and is for this reason basically unnatural) can be presupposed c. 150 A.D. only in Rome and Asia Minor, while there was otherwise only one Gospel, Tatian was probably the first in 172 A.D. to bring a combination of all four Gospels into the Orient (↗ 33 n.38). Starting from his native Assyria the Diatessaron must have been accepted throughout the whole Eastern Aramaic area in the first half of the 3rd cent. A.D. Despite its ascetical and anti-semitic tendencies any further translation of the Gospels was for the time being unnecessary and pointless. Since, however, on the one hand, Bishop Aitallaha of Edessa (324–346 A.D.) cites the Vetus Syra as an official Edessene text, and, on the other, the two surviving manuscripts, Sinaiticus and Curetonianus (A. Smith Lewis, *The Old Syriac Gospels or Evangelion da-Mepharreshe*, London 1910, reprint 1974; 4th and 5th cent. A.D.), contain alongside Old Syriac much that is un-Syriac (which the copyists tended gradually to eliminate: → 156), the Vetus Syra must have been transposed into Old Syriac from another Aramaic dialect in the 3rd cent. A.D., at a time when the Diatessaron stood unchallenged, so that many Diatessaron readings penetrated the Vetus Syra manuscripts. In this case it must have had its origin as early as c. 200 A.D. and probably in western Syria/northern Palestine (Antioch?, Damascus?). This was not only a Western Aramaic area (↗ 11) outside the region of early influence of the Eastern Aramaic Diatessaron, but also it is in this area that the canon of the four Gospels can first be expected to appear in the Aramaic region. Also the Vetus Syra exhibits clear Western Aramaic influence and in addition (in contrast with the Christian Palestinian translation of the Bible) an excellent knowledge of the Aramaic name-forms of Palestine. Eusebius († 339/40), Epiphanius († 403) and Jerome († 420) all knew of an Aramaic Gospel in use among Palestinian Christians and available in the library of Caesarea. Cf. K. Beyer, *ZDMG* 116 (1966), 248–252; A. Vööbus (↗ 33 n.38) 67–88; B. M. Metzger (↗ ibd.) 36–48; A. F. J. Klijn, "Patristic Evidence for Jewish Christian and Aramaic Gospel Tradition", in: *Festschrift M. Black*, Cambridge 1979, 169–177.

long final vowels (disappeared c. 100 B.C.; → 122) and is already attested to in c. 170 B.C. by the oldest Enoch manuscript, it must have become a written language c. 200 B.C. Confirming the same date is the fact that it did not derive from Achaemenid Imperial Aramaic, which was demonstrably still in use in the first half of the 3rd cent. B.C., at least in the whole of southern Palestine, as the ostraca from el-Kōm near Hebron (277 B.C.; L.T.Geraty, *BASOR* 220 [1975], 55–61, with A.Skaist, *IEJ* 28 [1978], 106–108), Samaria and Gaza and the inscription from Kerak show (J.Naveh [↗ 10 n.] 44, 50 and Bulletin 1974, 140), and which was first replaced in northern Palestine and Syria-Mesopotamia by Greek.[47] The place of origin of Old Palestinian could be neither Judaea (since Achaemenid Imperial Aramaic prevailed there until the middle of the 2nd cent. B.C. [Daniel; oldest manuscript of the astronomical Enoch] and Hasmonaean from 142 B.C.), nor Samaria (since then, at least in Samaritan, *ʾ h ḥ ʿ* could not have been written correctly from an etymological point of view: ↗ 39), nor Galilee (since the sole normal imperative and perfect afformatives in the oldest inscriptions, *-ī́n -ū́n -ẹ́n -ọ́n,* suggest that the written language of Galilee arose after their appearance: ↗ 39; → 99). Hence only the East Jordan area remains and quite likely the northern part (Paneas-Caesarea Philippi?), since there the Achaemenid Imperial Aramaic of Jerusalem and Judaea was furthest away and northern Old Eastern Aramaic (↗ 31) and Babylonia (→ 230) were at their nearest. In Old Palestinian the demonstratives lengthened with *hā-* do not yet appear (→ 151).

Otherwise Old Western Aramaic is indirectly attested to in the Aramaisms in Hebrew[48] and in the Septuagint, in Josephus and in the

---

[47] The gap between the introduction of the written language and its first appearance in the actual evidence amounts to more than 200 years in the case of Nabataean, around 200 years in the case of Hebrew (from the beginning of the monarchy to 800 B.C.), at least 150 years in the case of Ancient Aramaic, 138 in the case of Syriac, about 120 years in Carthage (825 B.C. to *KAI* 73) and in the case of Greek (↗ 59) and at most a few years in the cases of Achaemenid Imperial Aramaic, Hasmonaean and Jewish Old Palestinian.

[48] E.Y.Kutscher, *A History of the Hebrew Language,* Jerusalem 1982; M.Wagner, *Die lexikalischen und grammatikalischen Aramaismen im alttestamentlichen Hebräisch,* Berlin 1966, with my review in *ZDMG* 120 (1970), 195–198; A.Kropat, *Die Syntax des Autors der Chronik,* Gießen 1909; R.Polzin, *Late Biblical Hebrew,* Missoula 1976; E. Qimron, *The Hebrew of the Dead Sea Scrolls,* Cambridge/Mass. 1986; *The Historical Dictionary of the Hebrew Language,* vol. 1 (Concordance of post-Biblical Hebrew: Sir,

New Testament,[49] in the traces of Western Aramaic in Hasmonaean (↗ 21), in the historical orthography of Jewish Middle Palestinian and of Samaritan and in the Middle and Modern Aramaic continuation of Old Western Aramaic including modern place-names.

Taking all the sources mentioned together, seven different Western Aramaic dialects can be clearly distinguished at the time of Jesus; of course the approximately three million Aramaeans of Palestine and western Syria[50] could always understand each other.

Judaean, the dialect of Jerusalem and Judaea, is represented by Old Judaean (↗ 35; 37 B.C. – 135 A.D.) with its Middle Judaean continuation (↗ 49; from 200 A.D.), those components of Biblical Aramaic (↗ 19) and of Hasmonaean (↗ 21) which diverge from Achaemenid Imperial Aramaic, the pronunciation of Hebrew of the Septuagint, which originated in neighbouring Egypt, the Aramaisms of the Neo-Hebrew documents of the Dead Sea (↗ 43; 132–135 A.D.) and the Aramaic names from Judaea. Surprisingly the words of Jesus transmitted in Aramaic in the New Testament (→ 117, 123) also belong here, indicating that the traditions about Jesus did not come into the Greek-speaking environment directly from Galilee but by way of Jerusalem: even if there had indeed been a separate early Christian community in Galilee, it did not in any case send out missionaries. In Judaean *y* sometimes became ʾ between a long and a long or short vowel (→ 418), *aw* always > *ǭ* and *ay* > *ẹ̄* (→ 117), the

---

Dead Sea texts, inscriptions, Tannaitic literature), Jerusalem 1986 (microfiche); Dalman 10f.; Strack-Stemberger 104–106.

[49] Dalman; id., *Die Worte Jesu*, 2nd ed., Leipzig 1930, reprint 1965; id., *Jesus-Jeschua*, Leipzig 1922, reprint 1967; M. Black, *An Aramaic Approach to the Gospels and Acts*, 3rd ed., Oxford 1967 = *Die Muttersprache Jesu. Das Aramäische der Evangelien und der Apostelgeschichte*, Stuttgart 1982; K. Beyer (↗ 8) + *Festschrift K. G. Kuhn*, Göttingen 1971, 83 n. 19; J. A. Fitzmyer, *Essays on the Semitic Background of the New Testament*, London 1971; id., *A Wandering Aramean. Collected Aramaic Essays*, Missoula 1979; id., *To Advance the Gospel. New Testament Studies*, New York, 1981; E. C. Maloney, *Semitic Interference in Marcan Syntax*, Chico 1981; M. Wilcox, "Semitisms in the New Testament", in: *Aufstieg und Niedergang der römischen Welt II 25.2*, Berlin 1984, 978–1029; M. Reiser, *Syntax und Stil des Markusevangeliums*, Tübingen 1984; S. Thompson, *The Apocalypse and Semitic Syntax*, Cambridge 1985.

[50] J. Scheckenhofer, *Die Bevölkerung Palästinas um die Wende der Zeiten. Versuch einer Statistik*, Munich 1978 (about 1,750,000); M. Broshi, "The Population of Western Palestine in the Roman-Byzantine Period", *BASOR* 236 (1979), 1–10 (about 1,000,000); Y. Shiloh, "The Population of Iron Age Palestine", *BASOR* 239 (1980), 25–35 (about 500,000).

plur. suffix for "his" is *-ọ́y* (→ 118 n. 1) and the suffix *-ī́*, "my", had received the stress (→ 144), while the other old unaccented long final vowels had disappeared (→ 122). The accusative particle *yā̀ṯ* is common.

South-east Judaean, the dialect of Engedi and its area, is clearly distinct from the rest of Judaean in one particular point: the plural suffix for "his" is *-ọ́h* (↗ 21, → 118 n. 1) and "his brother" is *ʾaḥū́h*.

Samarian, the dialect of Samaria, is known primarily from the Samaritan of Middle Aramaic (↗ 50; from 6th cent. A. D.) and its influence on Samaritan Hebrew. As the Samarian-influenced pronunciation of the Hebrew Qumran texts shows (from 2nd cent. B.C.), already before the time of Christ *h ḥ* ʿ had become ʾ (→ 103); otherwise *aw* always became *ọ̄* and *ay* > *ẹ̄*, and between vowels *y* > ʾ; the plur. suffix for "his" is *-ọ́* and the 2nd fem. sing. imperfect has amalgamated with the masculine. In the numerals 200 to 900, "hundred" is in the plural. The separate possessive pronoun is *dīḏ-* and *dīl-*.

Galilean, the dialect of Jesus, is known from Galilean place-names, Middle Aramaic inscriptions (from 200 A. D.) and the rabbinic literature (↗ 47), as well as the Galilean parts of Galilean Targumic (↗ 24) and the Palestinian private documents from the Cairo Geniza (↗ 49), and the Galilean influence on the later traditions of pronunciation of Hebrew. In contrast with Judaean, Samarian and East Jordanian (cf. Mt 26:73; Mk 14:70), *aw* and *ay* are maintained in open syllables (→ 118), the afformatives of the perfect and imperative: *-ū -ā -ī* (→ 469, 473) had been replaced (↗ 25, 37, → 123 f.) by the corresponding endings of the pronoun (→ 423 f.), perfect (→ 469) and imperfect (→ 471): *-ū́n* (masc. plur., also for fem.) *-ẹ́n* (fem. plur.) *-ī́n* (imperative fem. sing.), and *-áw* and *-ī́w* (→ 490, 491, 494) had been replaced by *-ọ́n* (masc. plur. of III*ī*) though conversely the ending *-áyn* > *áy* (↗ 25, → 118, 149). As otherwise still surviving only in Samaritan, "hundred" in 200 to 900 is in the plural (↗ 25). The gutturals are articulated weakly (→ 122). The suffix *-ī́*, "my", is accented (→ 144). The plur. suffix for "his" is *-ọ́y* (→ 118 n. 1); the separate possessive pronoun is always *dīḏ-* (for *dīl-*; → 552). Also the replacement of the 1st sing. imperfect preformative by the 1st plur. form (↗ 25, → 152) might go back to Jesus' time.

East Jordanian, the dialect spoken east of the Jordan, is known from Jewish Old East Jordanian (↗ 35; c. 170 B.C.), Pagan Old East

Jordanian (↗ 35; 7/6 B.C.), a Christian Old East Jordanian dialect (?; ↗ 36; c. 200 A.D.), Jewish Middle East Jordanian (↗ 50; 3rd–6th cent. A.D.) and above all from Christian Palestinian (↗ 53; from 6th cent. A.D.). All unaccented long final vowels, including, at least in the south, the suffix *-ī*, "my", had been lost, *aw* had always become *ọ̄* and *ay* > *ẹ̄* and sometimes *y* > *ʾ* between vowels. The plur. suffix for "his" is *-ọ́y*. Characteristic is בוש, "evil, evildoing" (→ 528).

Damascene Aramaic, the dialect of Damascus and the Antilebanon, has to be deduced from Modern Western Aramaic (↗ 55, → 137), apart from a few Greek transcriptions (→ 118): as in Galilean *aw* and *ay* were retained in open syllables, the suffix *-ī́*, "my", is accented, the separate possessive pronoun is *dīḏ-* and in the imperfect the 1st plur. preformative replaces that of the 1st sing. The ending of the masc. plur. emphatic is mostly *-āyā́*,[51] the plur. suffix for "his" is probably *-ọ́h* and, as in Samarian, the 2nd sing. fem. imperfect has amalgamated with the masculine.

Orontes Aramaic, the dialect spoken east and west of the Orontes as far as Aleppo (↗ 11), is known only from a few Greek transcriptions (see also →121) and modern place-names (↗ 40 n.51): as in Damascene Aramaic the suffix *-ī́*, "my", is accented (→ 144) and the ending of the masc. plur. emphatic is often *-āyā́*. However, *aw* always became *ọ̄* and *ay* > *ẹ̄* (→ 118).

If one bears in mind the fact that Greek too was used in the larger cities, it is difficult to see where Hebrew could have been still spoken in Jesus' time.[52] Since Aramaic had spread from the north into Pales-

---

[51] *-āyā́*, which originated from the usual *-ayyā́* (under the influence of the gentilic-type affix *-āyẹ̄*?) and is metrically similar, lies not only at the basis of Modern Western Aramaic *-ọ́ya*: A. Spitaler, *Grammatik des neuaramäischen Dialekts von Maʿlūla*, § 99e, but also alongside *-ayyā́* at the basis of the endings of modern place-names of Aramaic origin from (especially northern) Lebanon and western Syria: E. Littmann, *Zeitschrift für Semitistik* 1 (1922), 167–169; S. Wild, *Libanesische Ortsnamen* 107; ↗ 55.

[52] Already the Jewish military colony of Elephantine, founded about 580 B.C. (M. H. Silverman, *Orientalia* 50 [1981], 294–300) from Judaea (*yahūdā́y*, "Jewish", means primarily and at the same time "Judaean": hence the Aramaic back-formation *Yahū́d*, "Judaea") spoke Aramaic (↗ 18) as did also the Jews in Edfu (from 5th cent. B.C.; ↗ 15 n. 10). The numerous ostraca from Arad (between Beersheba and Masada) were written in Hebrew until 595 B.C., but from the 4th cent. B.C. in Aramaic (J. Naveh, in: Y. Aharoni, *Arad Inscriptions*, Jerusalem 1981, 153–176) like those from Beersheba (J. Naveh, in: Y. Aharoni, *Beer-Sheba I*, Tel Aviv 1973, 79–82; id., *Tel Aviv* 6 [1979], 182–198), Tell Jemmeh (near Gaza, unpublished), Engedi, Nebi-Yunis (near Ashdod) and Elat (J. Naveh [↗ 10 n.] 44; all 4th cent. B.C.). The original Hebrew name of Naza-

reth was Aramaized (→ 113). Middle Hebrew (from 400 B.C.) and the transcriptions of the Septuagint (3rd–2nd cent. B.C.) are strongly influenced by Aramaic (↗ 37). In Middle Hebrew the degree of grammatical incongruity decreased considerably through the influence of Aramaic. From the 3rd cent. B.C. on the Old Testament text was written in Aramaic script. Only after the dying out of Hebrew could the most frequent of the artificially extended Hebrew pausal forms (↗ 57), especially nouns in the absolute state, have been used also as context forms (i.e. not in pause) (*BLH* 233m; perhaps it is a matter of mechanical transfer from word-lists: → 410); this is demonstrated already for the 2nd cent. B.C. (→ 107 n.2) to the 1st cent. A.D. by the contextual writing of ירושלים *Yǝrūšalēm* (instead of *Yǝrūšalém*) in the Hebrew texts of Qumran, in the coin legend ירושלים הקדושה *Yǝrūšalēm haq-qaḏǝšá*, "Holy Jerusalem" (L.Kadman, *IEJ* 4 [1954], 165; 67–71 A.D.), and in the Masoretic consonantal text (Colloquial Punic ναδωρ, "he vowed" [alongside נעדער, *nadár*!], and σαμω, "he heard", within a sentence [*KAI* 175: 3,4; 1st cent. B.C.] seems to be a consequence of slow and unfamiliar copying-down in Greek script). Also possible only after the extinction of Hebrew is the un-Canaanite lengthening of short stressed vowels in medial closed and final doubly closed syllables, which the Masoretic pointing shows (only) at the end of a sentence (*BLH* 232h, 580t). The Old Hebrew feminines *ʾáttī*, "you", and -(*á*)*kī*, "your", and the 2nd sing. fem. perfect *-tī* (always shown before suffixes in Masoretic Hebrew) were replaced in the Masoretic pointing by the corresponding Aramaic forms of the period after 100 B.C. (→ 122), for the pronunciation of these Old Hebrew feminines fell into oblivion because of their rare occurrence in the literature, i.e. after Hebrew died out, since in a living language the 2nd sing. feminine forms occur no less than the masculine. The first Targums were produced in the 4th–3rd cent. B.C. (→ 274). At the beginning of the 2nd cent. B.C. Jewish Old Palestinian developed into a written language (↗ 37). Even coin legends (→ 329), the words on the tokens for drink-offerings and the offering chests in the Temple and the calendar of fasts from Jerusalem (↗ 35) were Aramaic. There is even a story of a divine revelation in Aramaic from the Holy of Holies (↗ 35). In all the Middle Hebrew (↗ 34 n.44) texts from Qumran (before 68 A.D.) the typical Neo-Hebrew particle ש appears till now only 5 times (otherwise always אשר), so that it is clear that Neo-Hebrew was not spoken there either. In the Neo-Hebrew private contracts and letters from the Dead Sea there are many Aramaic words and idioms (Murabbaʿat 42 is even more Aramaic than Hebrew), while Hebrew elements in the Aramaic texts are very rare (→ 318f.). Also, of the Semitic words cited in the New Testament from the Palestinian colloquial, none are clearly Hebrew, while several are clearly Aramaic: αββα *ʾabbá*, "my/our father", κορβανας *qǝrbāná*, "the Temple treasure" (the ending of the emphatic masc. *-á* becomes -ας), μαραν, "our Lord" (→ 124), αθα, "come!" (→ 124), Μεσσιας, "the anointed" (→ 116), ταλιθα, "the girl" (→ 95), Ναζωραιος, "member of a Jewish baptist sect on the Jordan" (→ 113 n.3); to this may be added the names joined with *bar*, "son" (→ 536), while there are none joined with Hebrew Βεν-, "son"; and also: Κηφας, "the rock" (→ 608), Μαρθα, "the lady" (→ 630), Σαπφειρα, "beautiful" (→ 718), Ταβιθα, "the gazelle" (→ 588). A fallacious exception is Ισκαριωθ which on the evidence of the names in 2 Sam 10:6,8 איש טוב, LXX Ιστωβ, "the man from Ṭōb", 1 Chron 7:18 איש הוד, LXX Ισουδ, "man of vitality" and Jer 48:24 etc. קריות, LXX Καριωθ, "towns", is to be understood as Hebrew איש קריות *ʾīš Qariyǭṯ*, "the man from *Qarayōt (a town in southern Judaea: Josh 15:25; *a/ẹ* > *i* before *y*)" (on Ancient and Imperial Aramaic *ʾīš* → 517), as the exegetical school behind DΘ (probably with the help of the Hexapla) had already recognized (Jn 6:71 א Θφ; 12:4D; 13:2D; 13:26D; 14:22D ἀπὸ Καρυωτου); for from the fact that the *ʾīš*, "(originating) from", which is also common in Neo-Hebrew (H. L. Strack and P. Billerbeck, *Kommentar zum Neuen Testament aus Talmud und Midrasch* I, Munich 1922, 537 f.), is not translated (by something like ὁ ἀπό: Jn 14:22D; 21:2), but is transcribed as part of the name, it follows that it was a foreign loan-word at this time like Hebrew αμην; the family (Jn 6:71; 13:26) of Jesus' betrayer must have chosen the Hebrew *ʾīš* instead of the Aramaic *da* or *mẹn* (→ 550, 626) in the designation of their origin for religious or political reasons, which might give a clue to the grounds for the betrayal. So also Murabbaʿat 94a:15 [Σ]ωφηρα and 103 a:1 Ασωφηρ transcribe Hebrew *(has)sōp̄ẹ̄r* (pausal), "the scribe" (before 135 A. D.) and the Samaritans transcribe the Hebrew הר גרזים, "Mount Gerizim" as Αργαριζιμ or more often with the Aramaic ending Αργαριζιν (H. G. Kippenberg, *Garizim und Synagoge*, Berlin 1971, 54 f.) and Rev 16:16 gives the Hebrew הר מגדון, "the mount of Megiddo", as Αρμαγεδων. Josephus writes, for instance, ασαρθα, "Pentecost" (→ 95), κορβωνας, "the Temple treasure" (→ 137). Also Aramaic are numerous place-names (→ 95, 117 f., 129 f.) as far afield as Μασαδα, "the fortress" (→ 130), and Μαωζα, "the city" (→ 319), in the farthest south of Palestine. The High Priest עקביה *ʿAqab̲yáh*, "Yahweh has protected (the son)" (Masada; before 75 A. D.) and the most famous rabbi עקיבה *ʿAqīb̲ā́*, "the protected" (from Judaea; about 60–135 A. D.) bear standard Aramaic names. The names joined with Hebrew בן, "son", come from no particular area and sometimes the same person is called בר on one occasion, בן on another (Frey 1351 f.; J. T. Milik, *RB* 65 [1958], 409; → 348) or both are combined in one name (Frey 1131, 1170, 1351); in any case the transcriptions frequently have βαρ, but never *bẹ̄n*: בן clearly does not belong in the normal names of the population at large but is introduced only for special purposes. Two Hebrew ossuary inscriptions from Jerusalem (37 B. C.–70 A. D.) belong to Aramaic-speakers, as their Aramaic names show: ... מרתא בת, "Martha ("the lady") daughter of ..." (Frey 1311); מרתא אמנו, "Martha our mother" (J. T. Milik, "Dominus Flevit" [→ 339], 98) and three Aramaic ossuaries give only the religious title in Hebrew, "the Nasiraean", "the scribe" (→ 345), as a letter of Simon bar Kosiba gives his title הנסי על ישראל, "the prince over Israel" (→ 351). Roman soldiers of Syrian origin could understand the conversation of the Jewish inhabitants of Gamala east of the Sea of Galilee (Josephus *Jewish War* 4:1:5:38; 66 A. D.). The Galilean Targum (in the first place Gen 31:11E) calls "Hebrew" ל(י)שן בית ק(ו)דשה *lẹššān bẹ̄t̲ qọd̲šā́*, "the language of the Temple" (cf. Mishna Soṭa 7:2: לשון הקדש). The Mishna (2nd cent. A. D.) presupposes that in synagogue worship each reading of the Old Testament is followed by an oral Aramaic translation (→ 273). Even the oldest Palestinian synagogue inscriptions (c. 200 A. D.) are almost exclusively written in Aramaic (→ 335). In Dabbura (Golan; 3rd cent. A. D.) the synagogue inscriptions are Aramaic, though the inscription on the study-house of Eliezer haq-Qappār is Neo-Hebrew (→ 396). In the Neo-Hebrew tomb-inscription 5 from the necropolis of Beth Sheʿarim (→ 390; N. Avigad, *Beth Sheʿarim III* 236; c. 300 A. D.), which contains many more Hebrew (mostly of priests and rabbis) than Aramaic tomb-inscriptions, so that one might think that Hebrew was still spoken here, we find לעולם בשולם, "for ever in peace", and בשולם, "in peace" (thus not a scribal error, but incorrectly learnt); only warnings to grave-robbers are never in Hebrew (→ 335)! Cf. also G. Dalman, *Die Worte Jesu*, 1–10, and *Jesus-Jeschua*, 6–15; J. A. Emerton, *Journal of Theological Studies* 24 (1973), 1–23. The Aramaic dialects

tine, southern Palestine would be the most likely spot. However, the extensive archive of the Jewess Babata from Machosa south-east of the Dead Sea (93–132 A.D.) contains Hasmonaean, Nabataean and Greek documents, but no Hebrew (→ 319). The Neo-Hebrew private contracts and letters found on the Dead Sea (→ 318, 350) come in fact exclusively from the Second Jewish Revolt (132–135 A.D.), which indicates a conscious reversion based on nationalism to the "sacred language" in the only form in which it was then still available. Hebrew had not been spoken in Palestine since 400 B.C. (↗ 34 n.44). Thereafter there had to be special reasons for a writer to turn to Hebrew.

Middle Aramaic

In the 3rd cent. A.D. Old Aramaic merges into Middle Aramaic (↗ 10). There is no longer a common written language: it exists only as Eastern Middle Aramaic and Western Middle Aramaic. For the first time the dialects of Middle Aramaic are so fully transmitted that grammar and vocabulary are known reasonably completely.

Eastern Middle Aramaic

Of the Old Eastern Aramaic written languages only Old Syriac (↗ 31) and Jewish Old Babylonian (↗ 33) have a Middle Aramaic continuation. Mandaic is a new feature.

In the 4th century A.D. and probably in connection with the effort to produce an authoritative Syriac text of the Bible (*Pšīttā́*), Syriac orthography was reformed to take account of some aspects of the changed basis of pronunciation. This so-called M i d d l e S y r i a c (literary Syriac) became the ecclesiastical language of the eastern Ara-

---

must already have been spoken for a long time in Palestine, since they already show considerable variation at the time of Christ's birth (↗ 38). It is true that Aramaic has survived to the present day despite Arabic pressure (↗ 53), but only among non-Muslims, i.e. among people of another faith, while in the first century A.D. it would have been a matter of Hebrew-speaking Jews in the midst of Aramaic-speaking Jews. The Phoenicians too (↗ 34f.) had their own religion. Hence it is improbable that Hebrew was spoken in any isolated area down to Jesus' time and it is in any case impossible that the scribes obtained their scholastic Neo-Hebrew from such a place.

maic-speaking Christians.[53] On account of differences of christology the Nestorian East Syrians (Nisibis, under Persian rule) separated themselves in 489 A.D. from the Jacobite West Syrians (Edessa, under Roman rule), so that Middle Syriac also split into a Western Syriac and an Eastern Syriac written form, each with its own script and pointing.[54] From the 7th cent. A.D. onwards Syriac was pushed

---

[53] Th. Nöldeke, *Kurzgefaßte syrische Grammatik,* 3rd ed., with an *Anhang*: *Die handschriftlichen Ergänzungen in dem Handexemplar Th. Nöldekes und Register der Belegstellen* by A. Schall, Darmstadt 1966, reprint 1977; English translation of the 2nd ed. by J. A. Crichton, London 1904; R. Duval, *Traité de grammaire syriaque,* Paris 1881, reprint 1969; C. Brockelmann, *Syrische Grammatik,* 6th ed., Leipzig 1951, many reprints; id., *Lexicon Syriacum,* 2nd ed., Halle 1928, reprint 1966; W. Jennings, *Lexicon to the Syriac New Testament,* Oxford 1926, reprint 1962; R. Payne Smith, *Thesaurus Syriacus,* 2 vols. and a supplement, Oxford 1879, 1901, 1927, reprint 1976; J. Payne Smith, *A Compendious Syriac Dictionary,* Oxford 1903, reprints 1957 etc.; *Konkordanz zur syrischen Bibel,* Wiesbaden: *Pentateuch,* ed. W. Strothmann, 1987; *Psalter,* ed. N. Sprenger 1976; *Kohelet,* ed., W. Strothmann, 1973; *Propheten,* ed. W. Strothmann, 1984; M. M. Winter, *A Concordance to the Peshiṭta Version of Ben Sira,* Leiden 1976; A. Schall, *Studien über griechische Fremdwörter im Syrischen,* Darmstadt 1960; S. P. Brock, "Greek Words in the Syriac Gospels", *Muséon 80 (1967), 389–426,* + Studies II–V in: id., *Syriac Perspectives on Late Antiquity,* London 1984; J. B. Segal, *The Diacritical Point and the Accents in Syriac,* Oxford 1953; J. H. Hospers, in: *Festschrift J. P. M. van der Ploeg,* Neukirchen 1982, 449–455 (research report on syntax); A. Vööbus (↗ 33 n. 38) 88–121; B. M. Metzger (↗ ibid.), 48–75; especially A. Vööbus 96 and B. M. Metzger 59 on the dating of the *Pšīttā*; *The Old Testament in Syriac according to the Peshiṭta Version,* Leiden 1977 ff.; B. Aland, *Das Neue Testament in syrischer Überlieferung,* Berlin 1986 ff.; I. Ortiz de Urbina, *Patrologia Syriaca,* 2nd ed., Rome 1965; H. J. W. Drijvers, *Cults and Beliefs at Edessa,* Leiden 1980; S. P. Brock, "Jewish Traditions in Syriac Sources", *JJS* 30 (1979), 212–232. An otherwise unknown, exceptional form of Syriac of the early 4th cent. A. D. (always א for *-ā́*; but: dot or circle as word-divider; no diacritics except on *r*: ↗ 52) is provided by a Christian amulet (*DISO*: "Waw"): J. Naveh and S. Shaked (↗ 33 n. 40) 62–68. For the later pagan magic bowls in colloquial Syriac (Proto-Manichaean script or Estrangela; 6th–7th cent. A. D.) cf. V. P. Hamilton, *Syriac Incantation Bowls,* diss. Brandeis University 1971; J. Naveh and S. Shaked 31, 124–132, 180–184.

[54] Pronunciation and transliteration of Syriac are today usually drawn from the reconstruction of the state of things before the dialectal division, i. e. the early Middle Syriac of the 5th cent. A. D. Hence the following pronunciation is arrived at for the West Syrian vowel signs (with reference to the sections of C. Brockelmann, *Syrische Grammatik*):

ܳ : *ā* (except in Western Syriac *kọ̀l,* "all": 56 n. 3)

ܰ : *ę* before ʾ at the end of a syllable, since when this was lost it was lengthened in compensation to *ę̄* (180B; → 138).
a before all other consonants, since it was here lengthened to *ā* (79 n.; → 138).

back as a spoken language by Arabic, though it remained widespread as an ecclesiastical language until the Mongol upheaval of the 13th cent. A. D. (↗ 54). Middle Syriac literature far surpassed all the other Aramaic dialects in its extent, if not also in its originality.

The two southern Eastern Middle Aramaic dialects, Jewish Middle Babylonian and Mandaic, differ in fact only in script. Jewish Middle Babylonian, in square script, is the language of the Babylonian Talmud (finished in the 8th cent. A. D.; MSS from the 10th cent. A. D.), which besides the rabbinic discussion contains also many proverbs and folk tales, apart from its Neo-Hebrew, Hasmonaean, Babylonian Targumic and Jewish Palestinian elements.[55] It also stands behind the Babylonian pointing of the Old Testament and the Baby-

ܶ : *ẹ*, when short, since it was lengthened by compensation to *ẹ̄* (31; 47bγ.δ n.2; 181 E; → 138f.).
ẹ̄, when long.

ܺ : *i* before *yy* and in isolated cases before *s ṣ z š* (4aβ n.1; 49; 55).
ī, when *ī* corresponds to it in Eastern Syriac; *-ī-* and *ʾī-* as substitute forms for vowelless *-y-* and *y-* (55; 73 n.4; → 134 n.4).
ẹ̄ in all other cases.

ܽ : *ọ u ọ̄ ū* mostly corresponding to Eastern Syriac; (-/ʾ)*ū-* as substitute forms for vowelless (-)*w-*.

ܴ : *ọ̄* only in the exclamation (natural sound) *ʾọ̄* (47d n.).

[55] L. Goldschmidt, *Der babylonische Talmud ... hrsg. und übersetzt*, 9 vols., Berlin-Leipzig-Haag 1897–1935; *The Babylonian Talmud with Variant Readings*, vol. 1ff., Jerusalem 1972ff.; C. Levias, *A Grammar of the Aramaic Idiom Contained in the Babylonian Talmud*, Cincinnati 1900, reprint 1971; M. L. Margolis, *Lehrbuch der aramäischen Sprache des babylonischen Talmuds*, Munich 1910; J. N. Epstein, *A Grammar of Babylonian Aramaic*, Jerusalem 1960 (Hebrew); S. Morag, "Some Notes on the Grammar of Babylonian Aramaic as Reflected in the Geniza Manuscripts", *Tarbiz* 42 (1972/73), 60–78; D. Boyarin, "On the History of the Babylonian Jewish Aramaic Reading Traditions. The Reflexes of **a* and **ā*", *JNES* 37 (1978), 141–160, + *IOS* 8 (1978), 129–141; M. Schlesinger, *Satzlehre der aramäischen Sprache des babylonischen Talmuds*, Leipzig 1928; J. Levy, *Neuhebräisches und chaldäisches Wörterbuch* (↗ 8) + L. Prijs, *ZDMG* 117 (1967), 266–286; M. Jastrow, *A Dictionary of the Targumim, the Talmud Babli and Yerushalmi and the Midrashic Literature*, 2 vols., London 1886–1903, reprint 1950; I. Löw, *Die Flora der Juden*, 4 vols., Vienna 1924–1934, reprint 1967; id., *Fauna und Mineralien der Juden*, ed. A. Schreiber, Hildesheim 1969; G. Dalman, *Aramäisch-Neuhebräisches Handwörterbuch* (↗ 8); C. J. Kasowski, *Thesaurus Talmudis. Concordantiae verborum, quae in Talmude Babylonico reperiuntur*, 42 vols., Jerusalem 1954–1983; Dalman 25–27; D. Goodblatt, "The Babylonian Talmud", in: *Aufstieg und Niedergang der römischen Welt II 19.2*, Berlin 1979, 257–336; Strack-Stemberger, 13f., 107f., 185–214; J. Neusner, *A History of the Jews in Babylonia*, 5 vols., Leiden 1966–1970; D. M. Goodblatt, *Rabbinic Instruction in Sasanian Babylonia*, Leiden 1975; A. Oppenheimer, *Babylonia Judaica in the Talmudic Period* (Gazetteer), Wiesbaden 1983.

lonian Targum. Mandaic[56] was adopted by the Nasoraeans (→ 113 n.3), a gnostic/baptist community (→ 162 n.1), after they had left Palestine (Jordan area) in the 1st cent. A.D. as a result of the hostility of contemporary Judaism and had migrated at the latest in the middle of the 2nd cent. A.D. via northern Mesopotamia (Harran/Charrhae) to southern Babylonia (Mesene, Khuzistan). There, to judge from the Mandaic script (the script of the 2nd cent. A.D. Elymais inscriptions is closely related to it: ↗ 29 n.) and orthography (↗ 30), their oldest poems were recorded during the Arsacid period and probably in Arsacid Aramaic, from which after 224 A.D. they were gradually rendered into southern Eastern Aramaic, which had meanwhile been adopted by the Mandaeans (↗ 30, 31). As early as 272 A.D. a liturgical collection seems to be attested. The main works were finished in the 7th–9th cent. A.D. The magic texts on rolls of lead and bowls (4th–7th cent. A.D.) are closer to the colloquial. All the Eastern Middle Aramaic dialects have a Modern Aramaic continuation (↗ 54).

Western Middle Aramaic

Western Middle Aramaic embraces Jewish Middle Palestinian (in square script), Samaritan (in Old Hebrew script) and Christian Palestinian (in Syriac script). Only Jewish Middle Palestinian continues a written language which has survived. In the 10th cent. A.D. they were all replaced by Arabic.

---

[56] The term "Mandaic" is derived from southern Eastern Aramaic מאנד(ע)א *mandá*, "knowledge", מאנדאיא *mandāyá*, "layman" (→ 93, 107). Th. Nöldeke, *Mandäische Grammatik*, 2nd ed., with a appendix by A. Schall, Darmstadt 1964; R. Macuch, *Handbook of Classical and Modern Mandaic*, Berlin 1965; id., *Zur Sprache und Literatur der Mandäer*, Berlin 1976; E.S. Drower and R. Macuch, *A Mandaic Dictionary*, Oxford 1963; R. Macuch, "Anfänge der Mandäer", in: F. Altheim and R. Stiehl, *Die Araber in der alten Welt II*, Berlin 1965, 76–190; id., "Altmandäische Bleirollen", in: ibid. *IV*, 1967, 91–203; *V 1*, 1968, 34–72; further lead amulets: A. Caquot, *Semitica* 22 (1972), 67–87; J. Naveh, *IOS* 5 (1975), 47–53; J.C. Greenfield and J. Naveh, *Eretz Israel* 18 (1985), 97–107. E.M. Yamauchi, *Mandaic Incantation Texts*, New Haven 1967 (68–152: Grammar), with M. Sokoloff, *Orientalia* 40 (1971), 448–458. K. Rudolph, *Die Mandäer I*: *Das Mandäerproblem*, Göttingen 1960, *II*: *Der Kult*, 1961, *Theogonie, Kosmogonie und Anthropogonie in den mandäischen Schriften*, 1965; id., "Die Religion der Mandäer", in: H. Gese, M. Höfner and K. Rudolph, *Die Religionen Altsyriens, Altarabiens und der Mandäer*, Stuttgart 1970; id., "Der Mandäismus in der neueren Gnosisforschung", in: *Festschrift H. Jonas*, Göttingen 1978, 244–277.

While Jewish Old Palestinian literature is predominantly Judaean (↗ 35), Jewish Middle Palestinian is almost solely attested through Galilean. The reason for this development is that after the end of the Second Jewish Revolt in 135 A. D., as a result of the expulsion of Jews from Jerusalem and northern Judaea, the Jewish scribes migrated to southern Galilee and also the Sanhedrin moved from Jamnia via Usha, Sepharam, Beth Sheʿarim (all three on Carmel) and Sepphoris to Tiberias. Jewish Middle Palestinian also includes, apart from Galilean, Middle Judaean (with the dialect of Engedi) and Middle East Jordanian.

Galilean is the dialect of Jesus (↗ 39). The Galilean written language was probably developed from Jewish Old Palestinian (↗ 37) as early as the time of Herod and not only after the Second Jewish Revolt (↗ 37 n.47). The oldest Galilean texts are inscriptions (c. 200–700 A. D.), mostly synagogue and tomb inscriptions and inscriptions on amulets (→ 371–395). They come not only from Galilee itself, but also from Carmel, northern Judaea (between Joppa, Jerusalem and Jericho) and the Decapolis (around Gadara and Beth-Shan) and this shows that Galilean had spread to a considerable extent to the south. Since these inscriptions, more than fifty in number, are preserved in their original form, they are the most trustworthy evidence of the living Galilean language. However, the main pieces of evidence are the Aramaic parts (apart from the Hasmonaean and Old Judaean quotations) of the Palestinian Talmud (completed in the 5th cent. A. D.) and of the haggadic Midrashim (Rabbōt) to Gen-Deut and Song-Esther (completed in the 5th–7th cent. A. D.). They contain many proverbs and popular tales in the language of the ordinary people, so that they are especially useful for research on the language of Jesus (↗ 38 n.49). However, besides Biblical Aramaic and Galilean Targumic (↗ 23–25), Babylonian Targumic and Jewish Babylonian increasingly influenced the texts after 1100 A. D.; also the later manuscripts produced in Europe and the printed texts contain many mistakes. Hence only the oldest MSS, principally those from the Cairo Geniza, should be cited.[57] Galilean is further attested to by the Gali-

---

[57] Palestinan (Jerusalem) Talmud: critical editions: A. M. Luncz, *Talmud Hierosolymitanum ad exemplar editionis principis*, 5 vols., Jerusalem 1907–1919 (Berakot–Shebiʿit); E. A. Goldman, "A Critical Edition of Palestinian Talmud Tractate Rosh Hashana", *HUCA* 46 (1975), 219–268; 47 (1976), 191–216; 48 (1977), 219–241; 49 (1978), 205–226. Fragments from the Cairo Geniza (from 8th cent. A. D.; partly pointed: ↗ 24

n. 20): L. Ginzberg, *Yerushalmi Fragments from the Genizah,* New York 1909, reprints 1969, 1970; N. Alloni, *Geniza Fragments of Rabbinic Literature. Mishna, Talmud and Midrash with Palestinian Vocalization,* Jerusalem 1973; in addition in articles (cf. B. M. Bokser, 159–163; Strack-Stemberger, 180). Few manuscripts (from the 12th cent. A. D.). For the rest of the Palestinian Talmud one of the standard printed editions must be used like the Venice 1523 (reprints 1924, c. 1950) or, more usually the Krotoschin 1866 (with line numbers differing from the Venice edition; reprint 1948). Translations: A. Wünsche, *Der Jerusalemische Talmud in seinen haggadischen Bestandteilen zum ersten Male ins Deutsche übertragen,* Zürich 1880, reprint 1967; J. Neusner, *The Talmud of the Land of Israel. A Preliminary Translation and Explanation,* 35 vols., Chicago 1982 ff. (complete translation); C. Horowitz, *Berakhoth,* Tübingen 1975; G. A. Wewers, *Pea,* Tübingen 1986; *Terumot* 1985; J. Rabbinowitz, *Bikkurim* (+ text), London 1975; C. Horowitz, *Sukkah,* Bonn 1963; A. W. Greenup, *Taanith,* London 1918; G. A. Wewers, *Hagiga,* Tübingen 1983; C. Horowitz, *Nedarim,* Düsseldorf 1957; G. A. Wewers, *Bavot,* Tübingen 1982, + *Probleme der Bavot-Traktate,* 1984; *Sanhedrin,* 1981; *Makkot/Shevuot,* 1983; *Avoda Zara,* 1980, *Horayot,* 1984. Otherwise see B. M. Bokser, "An Annotated Bibliographical Guide to the Study of the Palestinian Talmud", in: *Aufstieg und Niedergang der römischen Welt II 19.2,* Berlin 1979, 139–256; Strack-Stemberger 11–13, 19–21, 163–184. Midrashes (manuscripts, including fragments from the Cairo Geniza from the 10th cent. A. D. on; partly pointed): J. Theodor-Ch. Albeck, *Bereschit Rabba mit kritischem Apparat und Kommentar,* Berlin 1936, reprint 1965 (Gen Rabba; the best manuscript, Ms. Vat. Ebr. 30, is, however, only referred to in the apparatus and even then not always); H. Odeberg, *The Aramaic Portions of Bereshit Rabba I: Text with Transcription,* Lund 1939 (after the basic text of Theodor-Albeck); facsimile editions of Gen Rabba Ms. Vat. Ebr. 30, 60 (10th–11th cent. A. D.), Jerusalem 1971, 1972; L. M. Barth, *An Analysis of Vatican 30,* Cincinnati 1973 (249–270, the longer Aramaic portions); M. Sokoloff, *The Geniza Fragments of Bereshit Rabba,* Jerusalem 1982 (the Aramaic parts); A. Shinan, *Midrash Shemot Rabbah I–XIV. A Critical Edition,* Tel Aviv 1984 (Ex Rabba); M. Margulies, *Midrash Wayyikra Rabbah,* Jerusalem 1960, reprint 1972 (Lev Rabba); S. Liebermann, *Midrash Debarim Rabbah,* 3rd. ed., Jerusalem 1974 (Deut Rabba); S. Buber, *Midrash Echa Rabbati,* Wilna 1899, reprint 1967 (on Lam); for the rest of the midrashes one of the usual collections of Midrash Rabbah must be used, like the Warsaw edition 1877 (reprints 1957 etc.) or Wilna 1887 (reprint 1970); Z. M. Rabinovitz, *Ginzé Midrash. The Oldest Forms of Rabbinic Midrashim according to Geniza Manuscripts,* Tel Aviv 1976; in addition: B. Mandelbaum, *Pesikta de Rav Kahana,* New York 1962; G. Svedlund, *The Aramaic Portions of the Pesiqta de Rab Kahana,* Uppsala 1974 (without text). Translations: A. Wünsche, *Bibliotheca Rabbinica. Eine Sammlung alter Midraschim zum ersten Male ins Deutsche übertragen,* Leipzig 1880–1885, reprint 1967; H. Freedman and M. Simon, *The Midrash Rabbah. Translated into English,* London 1939, reprint 1961. Otherwise cf. Strack-Stemberger 257–273, 282–287, 289–292. A selection of Galilean texts is provided by G. Dalman, *Aramäische Dialektproben,* 2nd ed., Leipzig 1927, reprint 1960 (with variants); J. T. Marshall, *Manual of the Aramaic Language of the Palestinian Talmud,* Leiden 1929 (pointed text after the Krotoschin edition with translation and index); E. Y. Kutscher, in: F. Rosenthal, *An Aramaic Handbook,* Wiesbaden 1967, I 1, 59–69; 2, 52–76 (pieces from Gen Rabba Ms. Vat. Ebr. 30, the Palestinian Talmud and Lev Rabba); G. Svedlund, *A Selection of Texts in Galilean Aramaic,* Jerusalem 1967 (from Gen Rabba Ms. Vat. Ebr. 30 etc.; many mis-

lean elements of Galilean Targumic (↗ 23–25) and by marriage contracts and bills of divorce (along with material on marriage law) from the Cairo Geniza drawn up in the 10th and 11th cent. A. D. in Palestine.[58] It was also Galileans, however, who, after 135 A. D., transmitted and normalised the pronunciation of the Old Testament, so that Galilean is also, finally, attested to by the pronunciation tradition from the Secunda (originating in 240–245 A. D. in Caesarea, cf. Brønno [↗ 8]) right down to the Tiberian pointing (completed in Tiberias in the 10th cent. A. D., cf. *BLH, BLA*), supplemented by the occasional Palestinian and Tiberian pointing of the Galilean Targum, the Palestinian Talmud and the Midrashim.

Middle Judaean is the continuation of Old Judaean (↗ 35, 38). It is only preserved in a few tomb and synagogue inscriptions and amulets (3rd–7th cent. A. D.) from southern Judaea, principally the area between Hebron and Beersheba, the region where Jews were allowed to stay after 135 A. D. In addition there are papyri and an amulet from Egypt. These inscriptions (→ 362–371) differ from Galilean on several points: the 3rd masc. plur. perfect shows etymological ו- or no ending (→ 470); the fem. sing. imperative shows etymological י- or no ending; the 2nd fem. sing. imperfect of III*ī* verbs terminates in *-ẹ̄n*; the nominal ending *-ẹ̄n* is retained (מתין, "200"); שומיה (→ 135 n. 3), "heaven"; מא(ה) *mā* sing., "hundred"; לה, "not"; more than once א stands for *-ā́* and *-ā-* and ש for **ś* (↗ 36). The South-east Judaean dialect of Engedi and area (↗ 39) differs in one important

takes). Dalman; H. Odeberg, *The Aramaic Portions of Bereshit Rabba II: Short Grammar of Galilaean Aramaic,* Lund 1939; E. Y. Kutscher, *Studies in Galilean Aramaic,* Ramat Gan 1976; id., in: *Encyclopaedia Judaica,* Jerusalem 1971, III 270–275; Beyer (↗ 8); M. Sokoloff, *A Dictionary of Jewish Palestinian Aramaic of the Byzantine Period,* Ramat-Gan 1987; M. Kosovsky, *Concordance to the Talmud Yerushalmi,* Jerusalem 1979 ff. (*Thesaurus of Proper Names* 1985); the dictionaries of J. Levy, G. Dalman, M. Jastrow, I. Löw (↗ 8, 45 n. 55) and S. Krauss (↗ 14 n. 9). M. Sokoloff, "The Current State of Research on Galilean Aramaic", *JNES* 37 (1978), 161–167. From about 950 A. D. the Jews of Palestine (and Syria and Egypt) no longer spoke Aramaic (M. A. Friedman [↗ next n.] I 51).

[58] Marriage contracts: M. A. Friedman, *Jewish Marriage in Palestine. A Cairo Geniza Study,* 2 vols., Tel Aviv 1980, 1981 (on language: I 48–87); divorce documents: M. Margulies, הלכות ארץ ישראל מן הגניזה, Jerusalem 1973, 119–123; matrimonial law: ibid. 27–31, 64–67. Their language is a mixture of Hasmonaean (passed on through talmudic citations: → 324–327), Galilean, Galilean Targumic, Hebrew and Arabic. A similar mixture is found on the amulets and in the magic books from the Cairo Geniza (cf. J. Naveh and S. Shaked [↗ 33 n. 40] 215–240).

point from the rest of Judaean: the plur. suffix for "his" is וה -ọ́h (→ 364). The Middle Aramaic inscriptions from northern Judaea are Galilean or Christian Palestinian; therefore northern Judaea was re-settled from the north and north-east.

Middle East Jordanian is the continuation of Old East Jordanian (↗ 35, 39). It is only preserved in a few synagogue inscriptions and amulets, mostly from the area east of the upper Jordan (→ 396–399; 3rd–6th cent. A. D.), and is closely related to Christian Palestinian (↗ 40, 51). As far as we can tell it agrees with Middle Judaean in its divergences from Galilean: 3rd masc. plur. perfect and masc. plur. imperative written with etymological ו- (→ 470, 474); the 2nd fem. sing. imperfect of III*ī* verbs terminates in *-ẹ́n*; the nominal ending *-ẹ́n* is retained (אסין "healing", חזין, "seeing"); שומיא/ה, "heaven"; לה, "not"; rarely א stands for *-ā́* and *-ā-*. In addition, from Pagan Old East Jordanian (↗ 35) one still has שנת, "in the year", and מה *mā* sing., "hundred". The eastern Jordanian synagogues are also different from the Galilean ones in their decoration.

Samaritan is the Aramaic of the Samaria-based community of the syncretistic-Jewish religion of the Samaritans, in which, probably in the 2nd cent. B. C., the old antipathy to the southern kingdom reconstituted itself around a peculiar form of the pentateuchal text. Samaritan is written exclusively in the Old Hebrew script and is known from inscriptions (→ 399–402; 6th–14th cent. A. D.) and literary works, of which the oldest datable ones, the basic material of the Mimar Marqa and hymns, were written in the 4th cent. A. D. (MSS from the 13th cent. A. D.). There is also the modern pronunciation of the Samaritans, which comes from the last stage of Samarian directly before its expulsion by Arabic in the 10th cent. A. D. (→ 146), though it differs from the pronunciation of the Arabic spoken today by the Samaritans.[59] Written Samaritan is not linked with Imperial Aramaic

[59] A. Tal., *The Samaritan Targum of the Pentateuch. A Critical Edition*, 3 vols., Tel Aviv 1980–1983; R. Macuch, *Grammatik des samaritanischen Hebräisch*, Berlin 1969; id., *Grammatik des samaritanischen Aramäisch*, Berlin 1982; Z. Ben-Ḥayyim and A. Tal, *A Dictionary of Samaritan Aramaic* (in preparation). J. D. Purvis, *The Samaritan Pentateuch and the Origin of the Samaritan Sect*, Cambridge/Mass. 1968 (with 7 script tables); H. G. Kippenberg, *Garizim und Synagoge. Traditionsgeschichtliche Untersuchungen zur samaritanischen Religion der aramäischen Periode*, Berlin 1971; J. M. Cohen, *A Samaritan Chonicle. A Source-Critical Analysis of the Life and Times of the Great Samaritan Reformer Baba Rabbah*, Leiden 1981; R. Pummer, "Antisamaritanische Polemik in jüdischen Schriften aus der intertestamentarischen Zeit", *Biblische*

ut depends on Old Palestinian, as is shown by the writing of ה for -ā́ ↗ 21). In view of the etymologically correct differentiation in the scriptions of ʾ h ḥ ʿ, which fell together as ʾ in Samarian (→ 103), it cannot have been created by the Samarians themselves. The orthography and modern pronunciation are strongly influenced by Samaritan Hebrew (and vice versa). This applies especially to the long final vowels which have disappeared (→ 122). To this may be added the feminine marker י, originally purely graphic, which was taken from the Hebrew personal pronoun and the 2nd fem. sing. perfect afformative and transferred to the 3rd fem. plur. perfect (as in Syriac) and the 2nd fem. sing. imperfect to distinguish it from the identical masculine (↗ 39). In later texts artificial forms multiply. There is also an Arabic influence. Since the oldest Samaritan inscription comes from the 4th cent. A.D. (the oldest in Samaritan Hebrew, Frey 1186 from Emmaus, dates from the time of Christ's birth), it is probable that Samaritan first became a written language after the birth of Christ (↗ 37 n.47).

Christian Palestinian is the written language of the western Aramaic-speaking Christians. Almost all the inscriptions come from the region of Amman and Jerusalem (→ 402–405; 6th–11th cent. A. D.). Then there is a letter (→ 403; 8th cent. A.D.) to the abbot of the monastery of Castellion/Mird (inhabited 492 to about 800 A.D.). The manuscripts provide only translations of Greek texts, especially the Bible (with no unified text, as in the Galilean Targum: ↗ 24). According to script, orthography and language these can be divided into two clearly distinct groups: 1. fragments (6th–9th cent. A.D.), including all the finds uncovered since 1952 in the ruins of Castellion/Mird, undated and mostly palimpsests with Greek, Syriac, Hebrew, Arabic or Georgian overwriting; 2. books (not palimpsests), mostly of liturgical character, including a Nile liturgy, some of which are completely preserved and dated (1030, 1104, 1118, 1187 A.D.).[60] Christian

Zeitschrift N.F. 26 (1982), 224–242; J.D. Purvis, "The Samaritan Problem. A Case Study in Jewish Sectarianism in the Roman Era", in: *Festschrift F.M.Cross*, Winona Lake 1981, 323–350; R. Bóid, *Principles of Samaritan Halachah*, Leiden 1985; otherwise cf. R. Pummer, "The Present State of Samaritan Studies", *JSS* 21 (1976), 39–61; 22 (1977), 27–47; L. Díez Merino, "El arameo samaritano. Estudios y textos", *Estudios bíblicos* 40 (1982), 221–276; A.D. Crown, *A Bibliography of the Samaritans*, Metuchen/New York 1984. About 500 Samaritans survive today.

[60] C. Perrot, *RB* 70 (1963), 506–555, has brought together all the texts known so far and arranged them according to their time of origin. Since there have appeared: M.

Palestinian does not relate to any written Palestinian language (in view of א for -*ā́*: ↗ 21) but took over the letter-forms, including certain diacritic points (*r*, plur., suffix "her") and writing conventions, from early Middle Syriac (↗ 43; 4th cent. A. D.). In addition a reversed פ was introduced for π and later also a simple form of pointing. No connection exists with the Palestinian church, in which the so-called Vetus Syra had its origin c. 200 A. D. (↗ 36 n. 46) as is shown by the fact that the Hebrew and Aramaic names in contrast with the Vetus Syra (and the Syriac Bible translations) appear mostly not in their original form but transcribed from the Greek (for example, יסוס instead of ישוע for "Jesus"), even if a similar Greek text and the same Palestinian Aramaic lies behind both translations. Also it is demonstrable that around 300 A. D. in Beth-Shan and about 400 A. D. in Jerusalem Greek scriptural readings and homilies were subsequently translated orally into Aramaic by an interpreter. This does not necessarily mean, however, that no written translations were yet available, since in the Palestinian synagogues the rule was that the Targum was not actually to be read out, although a written Targum existed (→ 273). In any case the striking Graecizing of Aramaic names and the numerous Greek loan-words show that, already before the writing-down of the text, so fixed a translation style had been developed, dominated by Greek, that the Syriac influence which came with the adoption of the Syriac script could not alter it. When we take into account also the fact that the first inscriptions and manuscripts to be preserved are from as early as the 6th cent. A. D. (↗ 37 n. 47), it is clear that Christian Palestinian must have had its origins about 400 A. D. It experienced a first blossoming down to the 8th cent. A. D.; then the Aramaic-speaking church of Palestine went into decline, as is clear from the fact that its Bible manuscripts were passed on to other religious communities as writing materials. In the 11th–12th

---

Baillet, "Un livret magique", *Muséon* 76 (1963), 375–401 (6th–7th cent. A. D.); M. H. Goshen-Gottstein, *The Bible in the Syropalestinian Version. Part I: Pentateuch and Prophets*, Jerusalem 1973; most of the texts edited up to 1912 are reprinted in the *Bibliotheca Syro-Palaestinensis*, 8 vols., Jerusalem 1971. F. Schulthess, *Grammatik des christlich-palästinischen Aramäisch*, Tübingen 1924, reprint 1965; id., *Lexicon Syropalaestinum*, Berlin 1903, reprint 1971, with the glossaries accompanying individual editions; M. Bar-Asher, *Palestinian Syriac Studies*, Jerusalem 1977 (Hebrew; he is preparing a dictionary), with T. Muraoka, *JSS* 24 (1979), 287–290; A. Vööbus (↗ 33 n. 38) 121–131; B. M. Metzger (↗ ibid.) 75–82.

cent. A. D. there followed a second blossoming centred on Egypt, but now only as an ecclesiastical language, influenced by Syriac and Arabic and with many errors. The places where the inscriptions were found and especially the monastery of Castellion/Mird give an important clue to the place of origin of the dialect lying behind Christian Palestinian. It is the same area, northern Judaea and the region east of the Jordan, in which the Christians had become the majority in the 4th cent. A. D. It may be noted that Judaean and East Jordanian stand closest to Christian Palestinian linguistically (↗ 40). Since, however, Judaean had withdrawn at this time to southern Judaea and northern Judaea had been re-settled from the north and north-east (↗ 50), there only remains the south of the area east of the Jordan.

The 25 synagogue inscriptions from Dura-Europos on the middle Euphrates (244 A. D. and earlier) could be Middle East Jordanian or Middle Judaean:[61] י often for *ẹ*, *ə* in עיבי(ד)תה, "the work"; א *a* in יאמא, "the sea"; emphatic ending mostly ה; masc. plur. emphatic יה; 3rd masc. plur. perfect (including III*ī* verbs) ו-; אנה, אנא, "I"; אינון, אינין, "they"; suffixes ה, הון, הין; הדין, "this"; הלין, "these"; ד(י), "which"; כד, „when"; תרת(י)ן, "two", fem.; בנה, "sons", construct; בשנת, "in the year"; חמש מאה, "500".

Modern Aramaic

Modern Aramaic is the Aramaic of the present day: about 300,000 people, mostly Christians, Jews and Mandaeans in remote areas, still speak Aramaic but their number is diminishing steadily. American missionaries in 1840 even produced a written language from Modern Eastern Syriac, making use of Nestorian script and following Middle Syriac orthography, in which numerous printing houses now publish extensively and everyone then reads the texts in his own dialect.[62] In

---

[61] J. Naveh, *On Stone and Mosaic,* Jerusalem 1978, nos. 88–104 (no. 90 after R. du Mesnil du Buisson, *Syria* 40 [1963], 304–314); previously: C. C. Torrey, in: C. H. Kraeling, *The Synagogue* (The Excavations at Dura-Europos, Final Report VIII 1), 2nd. ed., New York 1979, 261–276, nos. 1–22; Frey 826–845; *DISO*: "Jud. Aram". To this time belongs also Frey 824 from Palmyra. ↗ 34 n. 42.

[62] R. Macuch and E. Panoussi, *Neusyrische Chrestomathie,* Wiesbaden 1974, in which xxvi–xxix is a detailed bibliography of Modern Aramaic; R. Macuch, *Geschichte der spät- und neusyrischen Literatur,* Berlin 1976; cf. also F. Rosenthal (↗ 8) 160–169, 255–269.

addition in Russia after 1917 the Latin script appeared on the scene.[63] The distance between Eastern and Western Aramaic has considerably increased by comparison with the position in Middle Aramaic (→ 99) and even the bigger Eastern Aramaic dialect groups do not understand one another. A closed synchronic Aramaic linguistic system can be studied only in the Aramaic of the present day and it is only here that all the fine details of pronunciation are known. Hence Modern Aramaic is indispensable also for casting light on the preceding linguistic stages of Aramaic. Sometimes it has even preserved forms which are older than those of Middle Aramaic. But even where Aramaic died out, its influence is still in evidence in the Arabic dialects spoken in those places today, especially in vocabulary[64] and names.[65]

Modern Eastern Aramaic

Modern Eastern Aramaic comprises Modern Western Syriac, Modern Eastern Syriac and Modern Mandaic. It survived principally among Iranian languages.

Modern Western Syriac (native term: *Ṭurọ̄́yọ*) is spoken mainly by Jacobite Christians from the Ṭur-ʿAbdin (around Midyat in south-east Turkey). It developed from the Western Syriac of Middle Aramaic (↗ 44) if not directly from the dialect of Edessa.[66]

Modern Eastern Syriac is divided into several considerably divergent dialects spoken predominantly by Nestorian and Chaldaean (uniate) Christians (who call themselves "Assyrians"), but also by Jews (who call their language "Targumic"). Before the bloody persecutions of the present century these people lived in the region encircled by a line joining Mosul Lake-Van Lake-Urmia Hamadan Baghdad Mosul. Modern Eastern Syriac continues not simply the known Eastern Middle Syriac of Nisibis (↗ 44; most striking is *ḥ* >

---

[63] J. Friedrich, *Zwei russische Novellen in neusyrischer Übersetzung und Lateinschrift*, Wiesbaden 1960, + *ZDMG* 109 (1959), 50–81; 112 (1962), 6–49.

[64] F. Rosenthal (↗ 8) 169–172, 269.

[65] S. Wild, *Libanesische Ortsnamen*, Beirut 1973; R. Zadok, Syro-Palestinian Parallels to Lebanese Toponyms, *BiOr* 33 (1976), 304–310.

[66] A. Siegel, *Laut- und Formenlehre des neuaramäischen Dialekts des Tūr Abdīn*, Hannover 1923, reprint 1968 (including linguistic history; the material is not always reliable); O. Jastrow, *Laut- und Formenlehre des neuaramäischen Dialekts von Midin im Ṭur ʿAbdin*, 3rd ed., Wiesbaden 1985; H. Ritter–R. Sellheim, *Ṭūrōyō. B: Wörterbuch*, Wiesbaden 1979.

ḫ), but also the Middle Aramaic dialects spoken east of the Tigris, since it also contains southern Eastern Aramaic elements (↗ 11; → 93, 103).[67]

Modern Mandaic is only spoken now by a few Mandaeans (↗ 46) in Ahwas and Khorramshahar (east of the point where the Euphrates and Tigris join).[68]

Modern Western Aramaic

A Western Aramaic dialect is still spoken today only in Maʿlūla and two other Christian villages in the Antilebanon about 60 kms north-east of Damascus, though naturally there is strong Arabic influence.[69] In addition Western Aramaic has been preserved in numerous place-names from western Syria and Palestine, names which are, however, more or less Arabized.[70]

---

[67] Th. Nöldeke, *Grammatik der neusyrischen Sprache am Urmia-See und in Kurdistan,* Leipzig 1868, reprint 1974 (including linguistic history); A. J. Maclean, *Grammar of the Dialects of Vernacular Syriac as Spoken by the Eastern Syrians of Kurdistan, North-West Persia and the Plain of Mosul,* Cambridge 1895, reprint 1971; id., *A Dictionary of the Dialects of Vernacular Syriac* ..., Oxford 1901, reprint 1972; K. Tsereteli, *Grammatik der modernen assyrischen Sprache (Neuostaramäisch),* Leipzig 1978 (including Modern Western Syriac), + *ZDMG* 127 (1977), 244–253 (classification); 130 (1980), 207–216 (*bgdkpt*), *JAOS* 102 (1982), 343–346 (emphasization); H. Jacobi, *Grammatik des thumischen Neuaramäisch,* Wiesbaden 1973; S. I. Sara, *A Description of Modern Chaldean,* The Hague 1974; O. Jastrow, "Ein neuaramäischer Dialekt aus dem Vilayet Siirt (Ostanatolien)", *ZDMG* 121 (1971), 215–222; R. Hetzron, "The Morphology of the Verb in Modern Syriac (Christian Colloquial of Urmi)", *JAOS* 89 (1969), 112–127; A. J. Oraham, *Dictionary of the Stabilized and Enriched Assyrian Language and English,* Chicago 1943; I. Garbell, *The Jewish Neo-Aramaic Dialect of Persian Azerbaijan,* The Hague 1965, + *JAOS* 85 (1965), 159–177 and in *Festschrift H. J. Polotsky,* Jerusalem 1964, 86–103; Y. Sabar, *A* (Jewish) *Neo-Aramaic Midrash on Exodus* (Kurdistan; 17th cent. A. D.), Wiesbaden 1976, with D. Boyarin, *Maarav* 3 (1982), 99–114; H. J. Polotsky, "Studies in Modern Syriac", *JSS* 6 (1961), 1–32, Y. Sabar, "The Quadriradical Verb in Eastern Neo-Aramaic Dialects", *JSS* 27 (1982), 149–176; id., *The Book of Genesis in* (Jewish) *Neo-Aramaic* (Kurdistan) ..., Jerusalem 1983 (with a glossary); id., *Homilies in the Neo-Aramaic of the Kurdistani Jews* ..., Jerusalem 1985; G. Krotkoff, *A Neo-Aramaic Dialect of* [Iraqi] *Kurdistan. Texts, Grammar and Vocabulary,* New Haven 1982; R. D. Hoberman, "The Phonology of Pharyngeals and Pharyngealization in Pre-Modern Aramaic", *JAOS* 105 (1985), 221–231.

[68] R. Macuch, *Handbook of Classical and Modern Mandaic,* Berlin 1965.

[69] A. Spitaler, *Grammatik des neuaramäischen Dialekts von Maʿlūla,* Leipzig 1938, reprint 1966 (including linguistic history); + D. Cohen, "Sur le système verbal du néo-araméen de Maʿlūla", *JSS* 24 (1979), 219–239; C. Correll, *Materialien zur Kenntnis des*

Appendix

The Origin and Development of the Alphabetic Script

The alphabet was invented by the Canaanites in Palestine soon after 2000 B.C. as a purely consonantal script. The letters were at first pictures of (easily represented) things whose names began in Canaanite[71] with the consonant for which the sign stood (acrophony). Then, still in the 2nd millennium B.C., they developed into abstract signs (though the original form of A H K M N O Q R T is still recognizable today), in the process of which some also changed their name,[72] while others lost their sense through changes to produce rhyming or through shortening.[73] The change from vertical to horizontal line orientation would tend to bring about a 90° turn in the letters (other than R) and the change of direction of writing, their reversal (since the pictures would have to face the end of the line in contrast with the Egyptian hieroglyphs). However, since in the beginning the writing could be in any direction, the different positions were combined. From 1050 B.C. writing in Palestine was from right to left and in addition it sometimes had word-division through use of strokes, dots or spaces. The letters hung

---

neuaramäischen Dialekts von Baḫ'a, diss. Munich 1969; id., *ZDMG* 124 (1974), 271–285; V. Cantarino, *Der neuaramäische Dialekt von Ǧubb 'Adīn,* diss. Munich 1961; G. Bergsträsser, *Glossar des neuaramäischen Dialekts von Ma'lūla,* Leipzig 1921, reprint 1966; C. Correll, *Untersuchungen zur Syntax der neuwestaramäischen Dialekte des Antilibanon* (*Ma'lūla, Baḫ'a, Ǧubb 'Adīn*), Wiesbaden 1978.

[70] Th. Nöldeke, "Zur Topographie und Geschichte des Damascenischen Gebietes und der Haurāngegend", *ZDMG* 29 (1876), 419–444; E. Littmann, "Zur Topographie der Antiochene und Apamene", *Zeitschrift für Semitistik* 1 (1922), 163–195; S. Wild, *Libanesische Ortsnamen,* Beirut 1973; id., "Zu aramäischen Ortsnamen in Palästina", in: *La toponymie antique,* Leiden 1977, 65–73.

[71] The letter-names *dágu, wáwwu, mā́ma, naḥášu, ǵā́ru* and *táwwu* are only known from Canaanite.

[72] Even before transposition into the Ugaritic cuneiform alphabet around 1400 B.C. *dágu,* "fish", became *dẹ́ltu,* "door", and *pẹ́'atu,* "corner", became *pū,* "mouth", (in the 10th cent. B.C. *pū > pẹ̄, ṣadū́ > ṣadẹ̄́, mọ̄́ma > mẹ̄m*: → 87 n. 1); before the Greek script branched off in the 9th cent. B.C. the imprecation "*họ̄*!" became "*hẹ̄*!" and *naḥášu,* "snake", became *nū́nu,* "fish"; and after adoption by the Aramaeans in the 11th cent. B.C. (according to the evidence of LXX Ps 119 + Lam and the Syriac, "Hebrew", Samaritan and Arabic names) σαν *šann,* "bow", became σεν *šẹnn,* "tooth", becoming after 125 B.C. σιν *šīn* (→ 106 n.); so also *sámkat* > σαμχ *samk* and through Aramaization *'ẹ̄n* > αιν *'ayn* and *rọ̄š* > ρης *rẹ̄š,* while βηθ ιωδ μημ φη retained their Phoenician form. Σῖγμα is Greek (from σιγμός, "hissing"). The most ancient Hebrew-Aramaic letter-names are provided by the LXX (2nd cent. B.C.; → 114 n. 1): αλφ, βηθ, γιμλ, δελθ, η, ουαυ, ζαι, ηθ, τηθ, ιωθ, χαφ, λαβδ, μημ, νουν, σαμχ, αιν, φη, σαδη, κωφ, ρησ, σεν, θαυ.

[73] Rhyme within Phoenician/Greek: *hẹ̄//ḥẹ̄t//ṭẹ̄t*//Ζῆτα//'Ιῶτα, Νῦ//Μῦ, (ῥῶ//μῶ//νῶ); within Aramaic: *bẹ̄t+ dẹlt//gẹml,* after 150 B.C. (→ 120 f.): *'ayn//zayn,* in Syriac: *pẹ̄//'ẹ̄* and the spread of the form *qāṭál* from *'āláp̄* and *lāmáḏ.*

on to the (imaginary) line of writing. As the name 'Ἰῶτα < *yọ̄d* < *yắdu* shows, the letter-names had the pausal form (the form used at the end of a sentence); however, on account of Canaanite syllable formation this is only distinguished from the context form (which is shown in the script table) where short stressed vowels (on Canaanite word-stress → 142 n. 1, 2) stand in originally open syllables so that they are lengthened in pause, either as in Phoenician up to the full length of a long vowel (so that *á* > *ọ́*) or only slightly as in Old Hebrew (↗ 34 n. 44) and the rest of South Canaanite (so that *á* does not become *ọ́* but in Middle Hebrew *ắ*: ↗ 41 n.): *dắgu, yắdu, naḥắšu, pẹ́'atu.* The usual order of the alphabet[74] is known as early as the 14th cent. B.C. in Ugarit and it certainly went back to the beginning, though the rationale behind it is not clear; in Ancient South Arabian it was rearranged (*h l ḥ m q w ś r ǵ t š b k n ḫ* ...) and, less dramatically, also in Arabic in the 8th cent. A.D. on the basis of similarity of letters. Letters created at a later stage, as the Ugaritic (*'i 'u ś*) and Greek (Υ Φ Χ Ψ Ω) alphabets show, were attached at the end in the order of their appearance; nor do they have any proper names. Forms, names and order of the letters belong together from the start. As evidence of Greek schooling shows, they were always learned together. Out of the Old Canaanite script (attested to in Palestine in the 17th–12th cent. B.C., importantly around 1500 B.C. by the proto-Sinaitic inscriptions and in the 14th–12th cent. B.C. by the secondary cuneiform version known principally from Ugarit which uses the simplest possible combinations of wedges: thus an angle wedge for a circle) there were produced by stylization a Phoenician branch (from 1050 B.C.) and a South Arabian branch (very fine, symmetrical and steady letters paralleled only by Greek; branching off c. 1300 B.C. and attested from the 9th cent. B.C.). The stylized script table (↗ 58) follows the Ugaritic order and provides for the cuneiform alphabet the beginning of the Ugaritic names as recorded in cuneiform sources, for the South Arabian letters the Ethiopic names and for the Phoenician the Greek names.

---

[74] The order of the alphabet is shown in the 14th cent. B.C. by Ugarit (27+3 letters), in the 12th cent. B.C. by 'Izbet Ṣarṭah in Judaea (22 letters; ע after פ), in the 8th cent. B.C. by Kuntillet 'Ajrud in Sinai (A. Lemaire, *Les écoles et la formation de la Bible dans l'ancien Israël,* Göttingen 1981, 25–27, 90; id., in: *Studi epigrafici e linguistici* 1 [1984], 131–143; mostly ע after פ) and by the Aramaic of Tell Halaf ('-*r*; *NESE* 3,1–9), in the 7th cent. B.C. by Etruscan (22+4), Greek (21+5), in the 5th cent. B.C. by the Aramaic of Egypt (*NESE* 3, 1f.; Segal [↗ 16 n.] VII) and by an Aramaic text of unknown origin (Bulletin 1979, 151); around this time are also the Hebrew alphabetical psalms etc. (*BLH* 66f.; sometimes ע after פ, only one ח ע ש). About 30 B.C. the order can be seen in the square script from Qumran (R. de Vaux, *RB* 61 [1954], 229), in 68–135 A.D. in square script from Judaea (J.T. Milik, in: *DJD* 2 = *Murabba'at* 10B, 11, 78–80; E. Testa, in: *Herodion IV,* Jerusalem 1972, no. 53 a.b.b.; E. Puech, *RB* 87 [1980], 118–126; J. Patrich, *RB* 92 [1985], 265–270), in the 2nd cent. A.D. in Hatra 14 and later in Arabic in use as numbers. Beginnings and fragments of the alphabet are frequent from the 8th cent. B.C. on, cf. Bulletin 1979, 2. On the South Arabian reordering cf. F. Bron and C. Robin, *Semitica* 24 (1974), 77–82; M.D. Coogan, *BASOR* 216 (1974), 61–63; J. Ryckmans, *L'Antiquité classique* 50 (1981), 698–706; W.W. Müller, in: W. Fischer (ed.), *Grundriß der arabischen Philologie I,* Wiesbaden 1982, 22 (Lihyanite). The alphabet inscriptions are partly school exercises, partly apotropaic magic. The word ὁ/ἡ ἀλφάβητος is not attested until the A.D. period.

Attkanaanäisch	Ugarit.	Südar.	Phöniz.	Lat.	Attkanaanäisch	Ugarit.	Südar.	Phöniz.	Lat.
Stier ʾálpu	a	ʾAlf	ʾAlφα	A	Wasser máma		Māy	Mū	M
Haus bêtu	be	Bêt	Bῆτα	B	Fluß dábu		Zay	Zῆτα	Z
Stock gámlu	ga	Gaml	Γάμμα	C	Schlange naḫášu		Naḥās	Nū	N
Knäul ḫármu	ḫa	Ḫarm			ṭ				
Fisch dágu	Dant	Δέλτα	D	Wirbelsäule sámkatu			Ξεῖ	
Betender „hō"	ú	Hōy	Eῖ	E	Auge ʿénu		Ayn	Oῦ	O
Haken wáwwu	w-	Yaman	Fαῦ Y	V	Ecke pêʾatu	pu	ʾAf	Πεῖ	P
záyyu	zi				Blume sadú	ṣa	Ṣadāy	T	
					ẓ		Ẓappā		
Zaun ḫôtu	ku	Ḥawt	Hτα	H	Schlinge qóppu	qu	Qāf	Qốππα	Q
Spindel ṭáyyatu	ṭí	Ṭayt	Θῆτα		Kopf ráʾšu	ra	Reʾas	ʿPῶ	R
Arm yádu		lῶτα	I	Bogen šánnu		Šawt	Σάν	S
Hand káppu	Kāf	Κάππα	K	ṯ	Ťša			
Keim šêtu	Sāt			Fell gáru	ḫa			
Stachel lámdu	Law	Λάμβδα	L	Zeichen táwwu	tu	Taw	Tαῦ	T

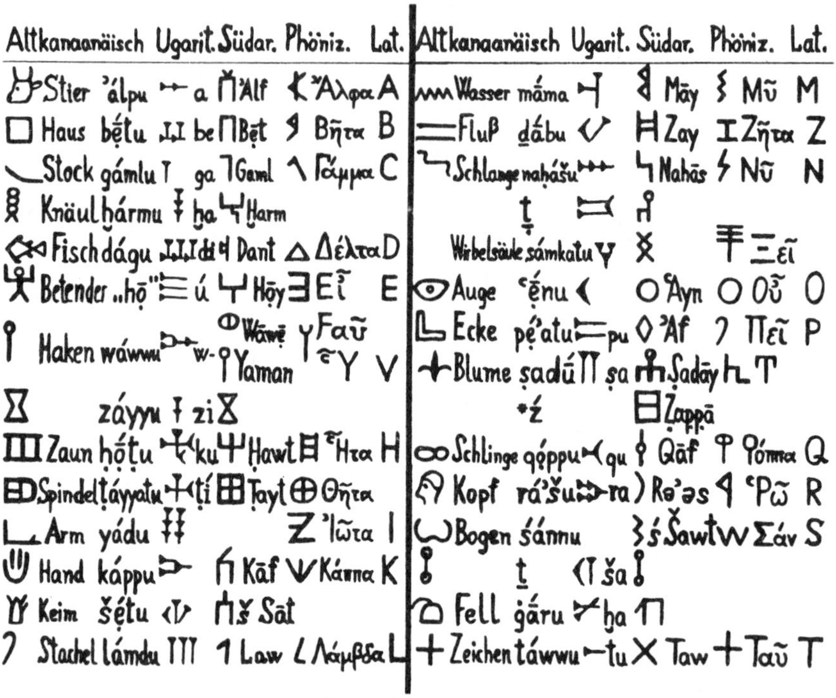

As the isolation of individual sounds is impossible to someone who is not trained in phonetics, the Old Canaanite script must have been thought of as syllabic, so arranged in fact that in contrast with Sumero-Akkadian cuneiform and the other syllabic scripts (knowledge of which would have prevented the creation of the alphabetic script) only signs of the form consonant + vowel were used and these were used not only for the first syllable of their own name, but also with all the other vowels, *káppu,* for example, being used for *ke ki ko ku* as well as *ka.* Correspondingly in the Ugaritic cuneiform alphabet (14th–13th cent. B.C.) the vowels *a i u* were exclusively represented with ', this being divided into three syllable signs *ʾa ʾi ʾu* (invented to better represent Hurrian) and in the older Greek inscriptions kappa is still used for *ka/e/i* and koppa for *ko/u* and in the Nikandre inscription from Naxos (7th cent. B.C.) H was used for *h ę he.* One can understand Old Greek KE in this light: the syllable *ka* is here to be read *ke* (A. Schmitt). As vowels are much easier to recognize as independent sounds than consonants, the existence of special letters for vowels is the precondition for being able to isolate syllables consisting only of a vowel (in Semitic every syllable begins with a consonant!), then the vowels as individual sounds and finally also the consonants. It was certainly the Greeks who first discovered, after the 7th cent. B.C., that vowels and consonants were the smallest units of language – one of the greatest achievements of human history. Thereby syllabic script became a script based on individual sounds, which it had always basically been, though not recognized as such. The Semites took over this discovery from the Greeks. If the deviser of the alphabet only writes consonants, without feeling that a serious lack, he must have been under the spell of a similarly vowelless script, and that can only have been Egyptian, which, writing all forms of a word with the same sign (since it is logographic), basically only records the undifferentiated consonantal framework. Hence the numerous Egyptian single-consonant words produce a complete consonantal alphabet, though this normally only served to clarify ambiguous multi-consonant signs by means of pleonastic writing. The inventor of the alphabetic script, ignoring all the logograms and determinatives, directed his attention only at this consonantal alphabet. He did not, however, take it over – it had in any case only 24 consonants – but created an analogous alphabet with the help of Canaanite words, though using multi-consonant words for lack of single-consonant words, with only the initial sound counting. This was a new concept in the history of writing. The 29 letters portray: bull, house, stick, knot, fish, person at prayer, hook, ?, fence, spindle, arm, hand, shoot(?), ox-goad, water, river, snake, ?, spinal column, eye, corner, flower, ?, sling, head, bow, ?, skin, cross-sign.

Judging by the Ugaritic cuneiform alphabet, c. 1400 B.C. all 29 Old Canaanite letters, i.e. consonants, were present in its original ordering except for **ź*, as is shown in the case of *ś* by a comparison with the Phoenician alphabet. Since these had been reduced to 27 by the 14th cent. B.C.: **ź* > *ṣ*, *ś* in Ugaritic > *š* and in South Canaanite > *ṯ* (in the 16th cent. B.C. at the latest; at so early a date it could hardly be a matter of '*ṯ* > *ś*), and to 22 by the 13th cent. B.C. among the established inhabitants (→ 102 n. 1): *ḫ* > *ḥ*, *ḏ* > *z*, *ṯ̣* > *ṣ*, *ṯ* > *š*, *ǵ* > *ʿ*, some of its letters had become redundant, so that the Ugaritic cuneiform alphabet wrote *š/ś* with the old *š* and the proto-Sinaitic script wrote *ś/ṯ* with the old *ś*, while the Phoenicians chose the old *ś* for *š/ś/ṯ* and for *z/ḏ* the old letter *ḏ*, though the name and position in order of *z*.

In accord with the fact that a script can only be improved if it is adopted by another linguistic community, which is unencumbered by tradition and habit regarding the form of writing and does not shy away from radical intervention, it was the Aramaeans who began, in the 11th cent. B.C., to use consonants also as vowel-letters (→ 409). Further, they developed from the end of the 5th cent. B.C. onwards special medial forms of certain letters (כמנפצ, sometimes also others) and from the 2nd cent. A.D. onwards distinguished letters which had become similar (→ 421) and, from the 4th cent. A.D. onwards, words which were written identically by the addition of diacritical points. From the upper dot to indicate a following *a* and the lower dot for all other vowels and lack of vowel were developed in the 5th–10th cent. A.D. for the Bible and the Koran ever more complex systems of pointing to fix consonant and vowel pronunciation (though only quality, not length), stress and tone. But what the Semites have never to this day achieved, a simple and unambiguous script, the Greeks had already created by the introduction of special vowel-letters around 850 B.C. (Greek inscriptions from c. 735 B.C.; ↗ 37 n. 47), as is proved by a comparison of the Greek and Phoenician letters Δ (still without a downstroke), K (already with a downstroke to the side) and M (horizontal).

The Phoenician alphabet as pronounced in Greek (ʽPῶ < *rọ̄š* < *ráʾšu* > Aramaic *rẹ̄š*, "head") is the original Greek alphabet from which all the Greek, Anatolian, Etruscan and Latin alphabets developed. The person who devised the script spoke a dialect which possessed *t* (→ 125) and t^h but no *ṭ'*, no *ʾh* or *ʿ* but a strong *ḥ*, no *y* but only an *i* and in addition *w* and *u*. So there were produced automatically from the recitation of the names of the Phoenician consonants the following Greek sounds (syllables): *a*, *b(e)*, *g(a)*, *d(e)*, *e*, *w(a)*, *z(a)*, *ḥ(e)* (later > *e* in dialects without an *h* sound), *i*, *k(a)*, *l(a)*, *m(e)*, *n(u)*, *s(a)*[1], *p(e)*, *s(a)*[2], *k(o)*, *r(o)*, *s(a)*[3], *t(a)*. The inventor of the script also made four decisions which are not self-explanatory: 1. Corresponding to the fact that he pronounced the Phoenician *Waww* in the Greek fashion as *Wau* (hence not *Wawwa*: →87 n. 1), producing *w* for Phoenician *w* at the beginning of the word and *u* at the end of the word, he wrote *w* and *u* with the same Phoenician letter Y: *Yαυ, just as he wrote the neighbouring sounds *k/k*^{h} and *p/p*^{h} each with a single letter (K Π). It was only later that someone else created a special sign Ϝ (digamma) from the preceding E to represent the rare sound-value *w*, while limiting the old Y to the more frequent *u* and placing it at the end of the alphabet since it was no longer the initial letter of *Wau*. The same principle of "one letter for one sound" also led to the creation of special letters for p^h (derived from koppa) and k^h (derived from Y or a cross). 2. The Phoenician *ʿẹ̄n*, "eye", which would have provided a second *e*, he defined according to ὀφθαλμός "eye" in Greek, as *o*, which was lacking otherwise. 3. The Phoenician *ṭ*ʾ (with ʾ following: → 78 n.) was selected for the similar t^h (with *h* following), though *q*ʾ was not used for k^h, which like p^h remained without a special letter of its own; rather, he left the two *k*'s (*ka* and *ko*: ↗ 58) and the three *s*'s (all three *sa*) alongside each other in his alphabet – an indication of how fixed and inviolable the Phoenician alphabet had seemed to him (though later only kappa and san/sigma were retained, while samkat was used for *ks*). 4. To those Phoenician letter-names which did not end in a vowel or *n* in his pronunciation he added an *a* (→ 87 n. 1). Only in this way could the Phoenician *pp* of *kapp* and *qọpp* be preserved, since in Greek there are no final long consonants. The double writing of long consonants and the first elements of punctuation (attested from 725 B.C.) were apparently invented first for Homer so as to show the metre clearly. From the Greek script there arose, basically without further alteration, the Latin script which is now dominant everywhere.[75]

---

[75] W. F. Albright, *The Protosinaitic Inscriptions and their Decipherment*, 2nd ed., Cambridge/Mass. 1969, + A. F. Rainey, *IEJ* 25 (1975), 106–116; 31 (1981), 92–94, + I. B. Arieh and B. Sass, *Tel Aviv* 5 (1978), 175–187 (*ṭ*), + M. Dijkstra, *Ugarit-Forschungen* 15 (1983), 33–38; J. D. Seger, in: *Festschrift D. N. Freedman*, Winona Lake 1983, 477–495 (Geser; 17th + 16th cent. B.C.); G. Mansfeld, in : *Kamid el-Loz-Kumidi*, vol. 1, Bonn 1970, 29–41 (in the 14th cent. B.C. *ṯ*?); F. M. Cross, "The Origin and Early Evolution of the Alphabet", *Eretz Israel* 8 (1967), 8*–24*; id. "Newly Found Inscriptions in Old Canaanite and Early Phoenician Scripts", *BASOR* 238 (1980), 1–20 (in the 12th cent. B.C. *z*); id., "Early Alphabetic Scripts", in: F. M. Cross (ed.), *Symposia Celebrating the 75th Anniversary of the Founding of the ASOR*, Cambridge/Mass. 1979, 97–123; Th. Nöldeke, *Beiträge zur semitischen Sprachwissenschaft*, Strasbourg 1904, reprint 1982, 124–136: "Die semitischen Buchstabennamen"; *ESE* 1, 109–136: "Der Ursprung der nord- und südsemitischen Schrift"; Bulletin under "Écriture"; R. R. Stieglitz, "The Ugaritic Cuneiform and Canaanite Linear Alphabets", *JNES* 30 (1971), 135–139; J. Naveh, "The Antiquity of the Greek Alphabet", *American Journal of Archaeology* 77 (1973), 1–8 (1100 B.C.); P. K. McCarter, *The Antiquity of the Greek Alphabet and the Early Phoenician Scripts*, Missoula 1975 (800 B.C.); A. Heubeck, *Schrift* (Archaeologia Homerica III 10), Göttingen 1979 (800–750 v. Chr.); A. R. Millard, *Kadmos* 15 (1976),

130–144 (1100–750 B.C.); E. Puech, *RB* 90 (1983), 365–395 (12th cent. B.C.); E. Schwyzer, *Griechische Grammatik I,* Munich 1939, 139–150; A. Schmitt, *Der Buchstabe H im Griechischen,* Münster 1952; cf. J. Friedrich, *Geschichte der Schrift,* Heidelberg 1966; D. Diringer, *The Alphabet,* 3rd ed., London 1968; H. Jensen, *Die Schrift in Vergangenheit und Gegenwart,* 3rd ed., Berlin 1969, reprint 1984; J. Naveh, *Early History of the Alphabet. An Introduction to West Semitic Epigraphy and Palaeography,* Jerusalem 1982, + *IEJ* 35 (1985), 8–21 (Philistine). ↗ 9 n. 4; 20 n. 14.